W9-DAX-086

Creative Strategy in DIRECT & INTERACTIVE Marketing

FOURTH EDITION

SUSAN K. JONES
Foreword by Mickey Alam Kahn
Preface by Richard T. Cole

Contemporary Direct and Interactive Marketing

Third Edition

LISA D. SPILLER
MARTIN BAIER

IJ IMC

International Journal of Integrated Marketing Communications
VOLUME 5, NO. 1 SPRING 2013

ARTICLES

Kelty Logan, University of Colorado at Boulder
Let's Make a Deal: The Exchange Value of Advertising

Lisa D. Spiller, Ph.D., Christopher Newport University
Using Metrics to Drive Integrated Marketing Communication Decisions: Hi-Ho Silver

William Ressler, Ithaca College
Integrating External Objectives with Internal Outcomes:
Benefits of Culturally Based, Holistic Approaches to IMC in Minor League Baseball

Stacy Neier, Loyola University Chicago and Drai Hassert, Sortis Internet Marketing
GREENOLAStyle: A Brand on a Mission

Victor A. Barger, University of Wisconsin–Whitewater; Lauren I. Labrecque, Loyola University Chicago
An Integrated Marketing Communications Perspective on Social Media Metrics

Amit Banerji, Maulana Azad National Institute of Technology;
Mohd Iqbal Khan, Barkatullah University; Mudasir Ahad Wani, Barkatullah University
India's New Language of Advertising: A Study of Change in Post-Libe

For subscription information, call Racom Communication
Or go to: http://www.IJIMC.com
ISSN: (print) 1943-3735; (online) 1943-374

RACOM
COMMUNICATIONS

2ND EDITION

The IMC HANDBOOK

Readings & Cases in Integrated Marketing Communications

J. STEVEN KELLY
SUSAN K. JONES

THE SOCIAL CURRENT

MONITORING AND ANALYZING CONVERSATIONS IN SOCIAL MEDIA

ALLIE SIARTO
RICHARD T. COLE

Foreword by
Richard Edelman
President and CEO
Edelman

RĀCOM
COMMUNICATIONS

Editor: Richard Hagle
Cover and interior design by Sans Serif, Inc., Saline, MI

Published by:
Racom Books/Racom Communications
150 N. Michigan Ave., Suite 2800
Chicago, IL 60601
312–494–0100/800–247–6553
www.racombooks.com

ISBN: 978–1–933199–42–9

CONTENTS

FOREWORD

The global shift in media, and how they are being used today, is having a dramatic impact on marketers, communicators and the businesses we support. Understanding the power of this shift requires recognizing the emergence of a new paradigm of influence. This book will help you do just that.

In this new paradigm the traditional pyramid of influence is replaced by the diamond of influence. The traditional pyramid of authority—CEOs, government officials, academics and experts—rests on top, with an inverted pyramid of community—social activists, action consumers and employees—supporting it. In the top pyramid, vertical communications—driven by mainstream media—dominates. But in the inverted pyramid of community, it's all about horizontal, constant, peer-to- peer dialogue.

The new paradigm replaces PR's historic emphasis on outbound messages from key influencers with dialogue—constant, horizontal, transparent and often peer-to-peer dialogue. Reinforcing the accompanying dispersion of authority is the "evolution" of the media industry—PR's historic means of message distribution. The rapid downsizing of mainstream media is accelerating while newborn digital news outlets such as *Business Insider*and and *The Huffington Post* are expanding, now having as many unique visitors as the digital versions of *The Wall Street Journal* or *The New York Times*.

Page views are no longer driven by catchy headlines, but by brilliant visual images and community commentary—a predictable outcome of a multi-device world where an average reader hovers at a site for only ten seconds or less before deciding to stay or leave.

Instead of spending thirty-five minutes with a print paper, readers now spend eight or ten minutes at most with a digital edition that is supplemented with news and information from several different sources. Today's average reader may have as many as eight total sources of news information. In fact, our 2013 Edelman Trust Barometer found that he or she might need to read, see, or hear something from three to five different sources in order to believe it. The impact of these *new rules* on the practice of public relations has been as enormous as it has been on the business of news distribution.

At the same time, the price point of digital advertising has fallen dramatically as *robots* are taking over media buying. Consumers now are able to time shift or otherwise skip advertisements, contributing to the tendency of more media outlets to move to "pay walls." And, in some cases, this strategy is working. Recently, for the first time in its storied history, *The New York Times* is making more money from subscriptions than it is from advertising. Simultaneously, many media companies are going straight to clients to generate a third source of income, offering attractive news-like content created by in-house advertising or PR units.

All of these forces, and others, are helping shift the communications paradigm from one dominated by persuasion to one best characterized by dialogue. And in order to participate in the constant conversation characterizing social media, a modern enterprise must decide to become its own media company employing various processes to convene and contribute to this constant current of conversation.

In order to deepen relationships and ultimately build trust with the various publics upon which they depend, enterprises are wise to practice what we call *radical transparency*. If the first phase of corporate social responsibility and organizational-public relationship building is about changing an organization's behavior to conform to public expectations, as we believe, a concomitant phase remains helping consumers change their attitudes and behavior to better accept the enterprise and its products. This consumer change, however, can only be expected when information is freely shared and enterprise trust is firmly established.

In helping brands navigate this ever-evolving and complex marketplace, public relations and marketing firms alike must help their clients develop their *BIG IDEA* through both insight and instinct. That big idea can be incubated and grow, and sometimes even discovered, within online communities. The big idea every successful enterprise needs can be articulated and supplemented with unique content that is brought to life through creative online enterprise newsrooms or through content channels created for these communities. The velocity at which the big idea is delivered and adopted can be accelerated through both paid and earned media.

The insights upon which the discovery, development, incuba-
tion and *viral-ity* of an organization's big idea may depend can
be enhanced with an understanding of the principles outlined in
*The Social Current: Monitoring and Analyzing Conversations in
Social Media.* In fact, I view this book as an important guide for
helping to navigate the historic change social media is bringing to
all of us.

Richard Edelman
President and CEO, Edelman

PREFACE

First, my co-author Richard Cole and I thank you for buying this book. We have tried to put it together in a way that will make a difference in your professional life, and we hope we have succeeded.

When I went to college to study advertising, I always thought that I would spend my career designing billboards and television spots. I never could have imagined how drastically marketing and other communications-related industries would change in just a few short years, and I certainly could not have imagined that I would find myself in a career that didn't even exist when I was in school.

College students today may very well be studying for jobs that don't yet exist, and the same goes for many practitioners who are already working in marketing communications, public relations and other related fields. Companies that fail to set up ongoing education and training for their employees today will quickly fall behind the competition tomorrow.

I started my company, Loudpixel, in 2009 to answer what I saw then as a developing demand for social media monitoring and analysis. Since then, I've seen the volume of social media conversations related to my clients jump by five to fifteen times.

Social media monitoring and analysis is no longer on the "nice to have" list for businesses and nonprofit organizations. Whether or not you're listening to, and in some cases participating in, the social media conversations that are happening each and every day about your organization and your competitors, you can be sure that your competitors are. You can also be sure that you're missing out on opportunities to discover who your customers are, what they really care about, what they think about your competition and how they are reacting to your offerings and marketing messages. You could be missing out on both opportunities and threats that could either make or break what the public thinks about your organization.

We can't begin to predict the direction that the marketing and communications industries will take over the next few years, but one thing is clear: Social media are not going away. Though the platforms will evolve, the number of conversations being shared each day in social media will only increase.

Though it may be safe to say that not every organization needs to have a specific social media marketing plan, we believe that every organization must have a social media listening plan. It's our hope that this book will lay the foundation to get you started.

Because new tools and case studies are coming out regularly, we've set up an online resource at *http://TheSocialCurrent.com* to accompany the chapters in this book. We encourage you to explore the site to keep up on the ever-changing world of social media monitoring and analysis.

Allie Siarto
Co-founder, Loudpixel

INTRODUCTION

This introduction tells you:

- **What this book is and what it isn't about.**
- **What principles guided the development of this book.**

Who Should Read This Book?

Perhaps you run a small clothing boutique and want to keep tabs on fashion trends for future product development. Or maybe you work in the marketing department of the largest bank in the country and know that your customers are turning to social media to ask questions, voice concerns and compare you and your organization to competitors. You might work at a public relations or advertising agency, and your boss has asked you to prove the value of your latest marketing initiatives and to help plan future creative ideas and digital content for a restaurant chain. You may work for a nonprofit that aims to promote healthy lifestyles for children. Or maybe you're a private consultant looking to grow your business. Fear not. We've put together a simple, actionable guide to walk you through what it takes to set up a listening program to:

- Monitor conversations around your brand and industry.
- Seek out opportunities and threats.
- Respond to customers around the issues that matter to you.
- Drive insights for creative marketing and product development.
- Evaluate what content is resonating with your audience and measure program success.

Stick with us and you'll be able to confidently navigate new opportunities and identify threats through social media listening and analysis in no time.

You should especially read this book if:

- You want to gain a better understanding around who your customers and potential customers really are and what they care about.
- You work with a brand or organization and struggle to understand what people are really saying about you in social media.

- You work on new product development within your organization.
- You support customer service for your organization.
- You are a small business owner looking to connect with customers online.
- Your boss has ever asked you to prove the value of your marketing initiatives.
- You are trying to create better content or creative initiatives for your organization, media outlet or personal blog.
- You work closely with social media for your organization already and need an additional resource to hone your skills.
- You are a student who is interested in pursuing a career in marketing, organizational-public relations, advertising or digital communications.

What This Book Is Not

No single book has all the answers. Here are a few things this book is not.

- This book is not a social media primer. We'll assume that you have some familiarity with the basic social channels such as blogs, Twitter, forums, videos, photos, etc.
- This book will not do all of the work for you. There's no "one size fits all" for social media listening. While we will provide you with relevant examples and stories throughout, you still need to put the time in to set your own goals and metrics, select your own tools and do your own social media analysis. Get ready to roll up your sleeves.
- This book is a practical guide to the social current. We're going to dive into real life examples, step-by-step guides and exercises. Have your notebook handy.
- While this book will cover *actionable* concepts related to measurement, it is not dedicated exclusively to social media measurement. It covers many other important areas of social media listening as well.

Social Media Listening and Analysis: A Real-World Example

When we set out to write this book, we knew that we had a lot to say about social media listening and analysis, but we also knew that we weren't the first people to tackle the topic. So what did we do? We ate our own dog food and analyzed a set of conversations about similar books to find out what people liked about the books and what they felt the books were lacking. We pulled a random sample of reviews from Amazon and tagged the reviews for context and sentiment to answer the following questions:

- What elements of these books are the most likely to cause high reviews?
- What elements are the most likely to cause low reviews?
- What types of people are reading books on this subject?

We knew that we could use this information to shape the content of our book. To start with, we found out the types of people most likely to provide reviews on social media monitoring and measurement books. We assumed, also, that Amazon review writers are more engaged in the material and also more likely to be in our target market. They are:

1. Beginners in social media monitoring.
2. Executives in various fields.
3. Small business owners.

The highest drivers of negative reviews of books about social media and monitoring were characterized by the following comments:

1. The book has a lack of actionable information.
2. The book title and overview don't accurately portray the content.
3. The book does not provide enough real examples to support the theory behind it.

We found that the highest drivers of the positive reviews of social media monitoring and measurement books by readers like you were the following:

1. The book must have real examples and case studies.
2. The book must offer a feeling of connection to the author or authors.
3. The book must include step-by-step, actionable guidance.
4. The book must be straightforward and easy to understand.

5. The book can be used as a reference guide for day-to-day work.
6. The book's product recommendations must be realistic and totally objective.
7. The book's content must be as evergreen and unlikely to become dated as is possible in this dynamic world of the social media current.

These positive comments became our Rosetta stone—a list of goals we could look to and tactics we could employ as we were putting material for this book together to make sure we were keeping the main thing, the main thing.

Our favorite line from all of the Amazon reviews we read became the overarching strategy statement for the book:

> Instead of having a bunch of vague ideas or a general concept of what to do, you should be able to find yourself saying, 'OK, cool. I can go do that.'

We hope that the examples and action guidelines we've laid out for you in this book will leave you feeling this way, whether you are a businessperson or a student. And we are planning that you'll walk away after you have read this book saying: "OK, cool. I can go do that."

1

Ensuring Better Marketing and Organizational-Public Relationships (PR)

Listening is a fascinating art and, when done correctly, it can deliver tremendous and surprising outcomes.

—Ram Dutt
CEO
Meylah

In this chapter, you will learn:

- How dialogue in the social current is powering modern marketing and organizational-public relationships.
- How good listening can develop authentic organizations.

Essential Terms for Chapter 1

- **Marketing:** The promotion of an organization, brand or person for the purpose of selling.
- **Public Relations:** Adjusting an organization's behavior to better conform to the values and expectations of a segment of the public upon which the organization depends in some way or ways, and then making sure that segment of the public knows about it.
- **Social Media Analysis:** The act of examining context in

social media data for the purpose of driving business deci-sions.

- **Social Media Monitoring:** The act of tracking day-to-day social media posts about an organization or person in order to capture ongoing issues and opportunities.
- **The Social Current:** The constant flow of social media con-versations taking place each day.

STEP 1—Understand This: Effective Social Media Listening Ensures Better Marketing and Organizational-Public Relationships (PR)

Before we get into the nitty-gritty details of social media monitor-ing and analysis, we want to take a few minutes to put what you are about to discover into perspective. Because even as we have promised that this book meets the goals of a "how-to" guide, we also believe that the strength of social media monitoring is the intelligence that it provides to an organization that takes the time to appreciate why intelligence matters.

What The Social Current Adds to Marketing and PR

Social media conversations and the data embedded in these con-versations have added new layers of both complexity and power to marketing and public relations. The social media culture is evolving so quickly that many organizations are struggling to deal with the opportunities and threats that come along with it.

To apply a little *diffusion of innovation theory* to the conver-sation, we can say that some companies have been *early adapters* to the new culture of social media. Of these, many have done so out of recognition of the great power of the information flowing in the social current. Others have adapted much more slowly—some only under the duress of tidal surges in the social current that have rocked their boats and created damage that they have experienced firsthand. As much as the social current is adding to marketing research, strategy and communications, it is adding just as much to the capacity to build and keep good organiza-tional-public relationships (PR). In fact, the social current is giv-ing public relations the long-awaited opportunity to create real dialogue with all the stakeholders upon which organizations depend. This is exactly the dialogue PR practitioners have hoped for since Edward Bernays, the "Father of PR," predicted that some day PR practitioners would abandon the one-way posture of the publicist and move to the "two-way streets" characterized by balanced dialogue between the organization and its publics.

From Persuasion to Conversation

The separate functions of marketing and public relations are often compatible and collaborative. However, they normally occupy different spaces on the chart of a well-functioning organization because they have different goals, objectives, standards and tests of performance. And it's important to understand these differences in order to fully appreciate and appropriately use the power of social media monitoring and analysis tools.

Marketing concerns itself chiefly with the development and execution of strategies to support sales. Marketing makes sure that products are capable of meeting customer needs and that they are priced right. Marketing identifies prospects for existing and new products and makes sure that existing customers are being satisfied. Marketing is focused on making sure that paid-for promotions are being delivered to prospects through media to which these prospects are attuned and that the proposition upon which the sale is offered is highlighted in that advertising. Marketing assures that the channels through which the product is distributed and displayed are open and effective. And marketing makes sure the people upon whom the organization depends to sell the products are well trained and reflect well upon the organization.

In the end, "nothing happens until somebody sells something," and the marketing department is chiefly focused on selling products in a manner that produces profit. And marketing has been given a great shot in the arm by the opportunity the social current provides to create dialogue with customers, retailers, suppliers, media networks and other stakeholders.

On the other hand, PR has a different and sometimes conflicting objective of building and maintaining relationships between the organization and the wide variety of publics upon which the organization depends. The effective organizational-public relations practitioner is constantly engaged in helping the organization recognize its requirement to constantly adjust its own behavior (which includes its products and services) to better conform to the values and aspirations of the stakeholders upon whom the organization depends for survival.

No business is conducted in a vacuum. Each and every day, a business is granted permission to exist by the customers willing to buy its products and use its services. Local and state regulators also grant permission to the organization to function, and these regulators have the power to restrict or withhold that permission within reason. Investors grant businesses the funds to grow, or not. Journalists, and their perceptions about the organization, influence everyone from customers to donors to government leaders. And lest we forget, businesses also depend upon the goodwill of its employees, its board of directors and its neighbors. Almost everyone is swimming in the social current, including the dolphins and the sharks. Social media monitoring provides information that may separate friends from foes.

Organizational-public relationship builders, like marketers, have also been given a shot in the arm by the opportunity the social current provides for dialogue with customers, retailers, suppliers and journalists.

Dialogue is key to both great marketing and excellent organizational-public relationships (PR). Two-way, give-and-take communication signals to all stakeholders that the organization desires an ongoing relationship with them. The messages the organization sends through its products and through the social current tells stakeholders just how much the organization appreciates them.

The Social Current: Powering New Marketing and Excellent Organizational-Public Relationships (PR)

Both the marketing function (which includes advertising) and the management functions of public relations have come to rely heavily upon social media to enhance their separate capabilities. Sometimes these separate capabilities and objectives overlap and complement one another. But sometimes they don't. Marketers tend to view social media as new vehicles to get product information to customer or prospect markets. Sometimes marketing communication is delivered through traditional media. Sometimes it is delivered through online advertising or conversations between the organization and its customers or prospects. Through social media conversations, marketers promote their products, and beyond that, they can learn about the positive and negative perceptions of their portfolios.

Marketers can also pick up useful tidbits about how their customers are using their products or services—whether, for example, their products are meeting customer expectations sufficiently to lead to brand loyalty expressed through satisfaction, intent to repurchase and referrals. They can react at Internet speed to criticisms or concerns that pop up in social media and turn a potential bad situation into an opportunity to create a lifetime bond. Beyond that, market research in the social current can lead to product or service modifications or expansions into new markets or territories.

Public relations practitioners, on the other hand, assume responsibility for making sure the organization is building and maintaining all stakeholder relationships. They develop and strengthen relationships within the communities in which the organization's facilities are located. They help management ensure that employees understand the organization's mission and have a clear line of sight between their jobs and the overall success of the enterprise.

PR practitioners develop and maintain relationships with the media gatekeepers who decide what gets published in the local paper or is shown on the "Six O'clock News" or printed in the blogs that cover their business niche. PR practitioners work with lawyers and regulators to prepare annual financial reports for the analysts who are influencing stock prices. And they assist the marketing and sales team in developing the strategy, tactics, events, brochures and videos—whatever is needed—to get company news to clients and customers at the right time. The PR practitioner also must take responsibility for helping the organization prepare for the various crises that may confront the organization or its executives. In fact, some say the most important role of the PR practitioner is one for which they almost never get credit: crisis averter. This is the PR practitioner who develops the kind of "sixth sense" that allows him to advise the business on how to avoid otherwise damaging crises. The social current is providing a new source of intelligence that transforms this sixth sense from the status of an instinct to the product of reliable and objective intelligence.

Producing Authentic Organizations

The PR practitioner must understand that the authenticity of the organization is the most important asset of any brand. Protecting the organization's reputation must take priority over the urgency of making the next sale.

Authenticity that builds a brand's reputation doesn't come from slick brochures or well-spun phrases. And, as we said earlier, besides building the image and promoting the overall interests of the organization, the PR practitioner recognizes that her most important role is to help the organization adjust its behavior to better conform to the expectations of all the audiences upon whom the organization depends for survival.

Social media monitoring—listening—gives the PR practitioner important intelligence in how organizational behavior can be reshaped to meet the requirement that organizations adjust and adapt. The social current provides an important vehicle for collecting information on needed changes, as it provides the vehicles for timely responses to stakeholder concerns in a conversational tone. And in these senses, and others, monitoring conversations in the social current provides intelligence essential to evaluating the degree to which key stakeholders and prospects view the organization as authentic and worthy of its respect.

Social media networks, and the information that is being shared through them every day, are helping both progressive marketers and effective PR practitioners create new ways of conversing with all stakeholders. This dialogue provides help to sales and marketing personnel, as well as to the organization's public relationship builders. Conversations within the social current can be translated into important intelligence for product planners, operations managers, human resources, government affairs and all external and internal publics.

Social media monitoring and analysis tools are giving both the marketers and the organizational-public relationship team a deeper appreciation of the different roles each plays in the overall success of the organization, and as a result showing them how they can learn to work better together.

Just the Beginning

You won't learn everything there is to know about social media monitoring and analysis by reading this book, but it's a good start. It should set you and your business on a course of much greater effectiveness, efficiency, productivity and profitability.

We can guarantee that the insights you gain by systematically *eavesdropping* on public conversations about you and your competitors in the social current will be valuable. Acting on the information you glean from these public conversations may make all the difference in the world for your customers and other stakeholders, your organization and to you.

Making Your Practice Perfect

At the very end of each chapter, you will find a section entitled *Making Your Practice Perfect*, which contains useful exercises that you can work through to take yourself further down the road of becoming an excellent social media listener. In fact, that's our goal for you.

When you finish this book, you'll be significantly more capable of being able to add value to any enterprise because you will know what to listen for in social media, how to listen and how turn what you hear into profit.

You'll develop these skills if you are a student studying this subject as part of a social media sequence, like the one Richard Cole has created at Michigan State University with the "New Media Driver's License®" sequence, and his Racom book, *Google This: The New Media Driver's License®*. And you'll develop these skills if you want to create a more profitable bottom line for your business, like Allie and Jeff Siarto do for the clients of Loudpixel, their social media monitoring and analysis firm.

You'll develop these skills if you work at it. But, like anything worthwhile you have learned in life, it takes practice to really understand and learn effective social media monitoring skills. And we don't want you practicing the wrong things, taking the easy way out, cutting corners or just thinking that reading the book will make you a listening expert. And remember this: Practice doesn't make perfect. Only perfect practice makes perfect.

There's a statement that some people attribute to Confucius:

> **Tell me, I'll forget.**
> **Show me, I'll remember.**
> **Involve me, I'll understand.**

We subscribe to this theory, and that's why we've decided to include the *Making Your Practice Perfect* section at the end of the remaining chapters in this important little book.

We're giving you somewhat of a pass here in Chapter 1. If you're reading this book as part of a class, it will be easy to take a look at each of the major points in this chapter and discuss them with your classmates. Remember: *Involve me and I'll understand.* If you are part of a business, large or small, that has asked all of the employees on a team or in a unit to read this book, it would be worthwhile for you to do the same thing.

If, on the other hand, you bought this book because you have a burning desire to be more successful at whatever you do on your own, it's probably going to be a bit harder to get involved with other readers. So we offer this option to you (and other readers who might be interested).

First, keep a notebook or an open a document in which to keep notes. Jot down the ideas you get from reading the book, highlight action steps you think would be particularly useful for your business or student group, write down words, phrases, business names or theories that you want to google later, and do the best you can to complete each *Making Your Practice Perfect* exercise we recommend, even if you're all alone.

Second, keep a copy of the book handy so when the time comes, you'll have the exact URL of our website (*http://TheSocialCurrent.com*). We've set up our website so we can interact with you in the future. More important, we've set this up so that you can interact with other readers who believe that if you're going to do something, then it's worth doing right. And that means that you need to have people with whom you can share your ideas, express your concerns, highlight your achievements and maintain professional contact because of your common interest in listening and learning in social media.

2

Monitoring, Insights and Measurement: What We Learn from Social Media

---

Effective listening is central to enhanced communication but managers do not always listen because active listening is not a natural process. It requires both mental and physical effort on the part of the listener.

—Marilyn M. Helms & Paula Haynes
Journal of Managerial Pyschology

In this chapter, you will learn:

- How research can be classified differently according to its purpose—formative or evaluative—or its type—qualitative or quantitative.
- How effective businesses and nonprofits use social listening to better understand the needs of their customers, and to uncover strategic insights.
- How organizations benefit from listening in on conversations in social media.

Essential Terms for Chapter 2

- **Evaluative Research:** Research that is intended to measure the impact of an action, program or strategy.
- **Formative Research:** Formative research helps develop effective strategies identifying the needs of target popula-

tions, and understanding how these populations express themselves. Evaluations that are used to measure the effectiveness of programs or strategies become "formative" if used to redesign these programs or strategies.

- **Insight:** A new understanding that will help to solve a problem or shape future planning.
- **Qualitative Research:** Qualitative research helps the researcher get a deeper understanding of groups, words or events by letting meaning emerge from the words of the participants.
- **Quantitative Research:** Quantitative research generates numbers that can be reviewed and analyzed statistically. Quantitative data are often collected with questionnaires or surveys, or in laboratory or laboratory-like experiments.

Finding the Perfect Tomato for Pasta Sauce: A Brief Primer on Purposes and Styles of Research

Before we go forward with our discussion of what we learn in social media, we have to say something about the "R" word— *research*.

Why the word *research* is so frightening to so many people is actually pretty easy to understand. Research findings, after all, are often talked about in a kind of academic jargon that seems, at times, designed to make us believe that only people with superior intellect are capable of understanding it. Nothing could be further from the truth. We "do research" all the time.

Here's a simple example: We want to figure out how to preserve the hundreds of tomatoes we plan to grow in our garden over the summer so we'll be able to have them to eat over the long winter months. We decide to do some research. (We call it searching or "Googling.") Research has been made so easy for us in the twenty-first century that we often don't recognize we are doing it.

Google the phrase: *How to can tomatoes?* You'll get more than a half-million hits listing everything from YouTube videos on how to use a pressure cooker to articles on how to can tomatoes without using a pressure cooker. This is research, and just on the basis of this single simple search, we are well on our way to coming up with a conclusion that best answers our specific question.

As our heading for this section says, we want to walk through a brief primer on basic purposes (formative or evaluative) and styles (qualitative and quantitative) of research. But before we go forward, there's one more point we'd like to make. That is the distinction between primary and secondary research.

As our colleague and friend, advertising professor Dr. Bruce Vanden Bergh, points out: "The Google example is really *secondary* research because someone has already done the work. You are taking advantage of that research rather than cranking up your own expensive *primary* research project, which would be research you would do because you couldn't find the answer in secondary research." For the purposes of our further discussion, we are going to mix some examples of primary and secondary research. You'll be able to tell the difference.

In the example above, one Google hit describes the best tomatoes to grow if your purpose is canning tomatoes specifically for use in making pasta sauce. That's even closer to the issue we are trying to resolve, and we realize that, most likely, there is no clear answer on that question. But in our *research* we stumble upon an extensive discussion on a food blog in which a dozen chefs in Italian restaurants are expressing their opinions on which variety of tomato they believe produces the most outstanding spaghetti sauce, and why.

Since our research goal is, quite specifically, to help us form an opinion that will influence the choices we need to make, we "tune in" to the blog discussion as if it were a focus group designed specifically to assist us in our endeavor.

We need a "tomato strategy," after all, and by following the blog posts of this "expert panel," we are using a research technique to help us *form* it. In fact, we're doing our research in a manner that is quite similar to the way modern political campaigns begin to develop messages that they think will appeal to the segment of the population they are trying to entice to vote for their candidate. It's also how automotive companies decide what accessories to build into their new models, and how to advertise them once built.

Formative Research

In the case of the chefs' blog conversation we are eavesdropping, in a manner of speaking, on an argument amongst a group of real experts on the subject. And we can use what we hear to inform our decision about which variety of tomato plants we choose to put in our garden. Our purpose is to use this information to form our "tomato strategy." We are engaged in formative research.

Formative research is done in a variety of settings and for a number of purposes. The California Department of Public Health, for example, advocates using formative research techniques to develop campaign messages that can help build social marketing campaigns to reduce accidents and lifestyle choices that lead to illness and death. (http://www.cdph.ca.gov/programs/cpns/Pages/FormativeResearch.aspx)

> Formative research is the basis for developing effective strategies, including communication channels, for influencing behavior change. It helps researchers identify and understand the characteristics—interests, behaviors and needs—of target populations that influence their decisions and actions. Formative research is integral in developing programs as well as improving existing and ongoing programs.

Back to our tomato example. We're reading the blog comments of a number of chefs in Italian restaurants because we think they ought to know something about pasta sauce, and we are developing the best "tomato strategy" to meet our needs. Even though it is quite obvious that the chefs engaged in this particular blog disagree on which tomatoes make the best sauce, we find their different opinions useful and meaningful. Some opinions will, for personal reasons, resonate more with us than others. That's OK. We are being selective and subjective and the purpose of our research does not require that we rely on a statistical sample of all the chefs in all the Italian restaurants in the country. We're doing our formative research using a qualitative research approach to develop our tomato strategy, after all.

Qualitative Research

We like the description of qualitative research provided by California State University, Long Beach (http://www.csulb.edu/~msaintg/ppa696/696quali.htm) in a data collection strategy paper they have made public on the Web.

> Qualitative research is aimed at gaining a deep understanding of a specific organization or event, rather than surface description of a large sample of a population . . . it lets the meaning emerge from the participants.
>
> Qualitative research aims to get a better understanding through first-hand experience, truthful reporting, and quotations of actual conversations. It aims to understand how the participants derive meaning from their surroundings, and how their meaning influences their behavior.

We really like the qualitative approach we are using to figure out what kind of tomatoes we should plant in our garden. We're enjoying the debate among the chefs on the blog, and since, in the end, the taste of pasta sauce is a very subjective thing, we're perfectly happy using a qualitative approach to form our opinion.

But suppose we wanted to form our tomato decision based on a statistically representative sample of chefs in U.S. Italian restaurants? We might not be concerned about all the qualities of pasta sauce that get bandied about in a free-flowing conversation among a panel of experts. Suppose we simply want to know if a majority of chefs in America's Italian restaurants have a particular tomato preference?

Quantitative Research

You can imagine that it would be highly unlikely we would have access and resources to run a major research study to resolve a question of what America's chefs in Italian restaurants would call their tomato of choice in pasta sauce. But the notion may not be as far-fetched as it might seem if, for example, we were under contract to the Prego Spaghetti Sauce brand to find the answer to this question. That company might just have a sufficient economic interest to want to get a much more robust answer than a focus group could provide.

To accomplish this task, we would use quantitative research. Here we'll turn to a Syracuse, NY-based blog called "The Research Bunker" for a definition.(http://rmsbunkerblog.wordpress.com/ 2011/04/01/what-is-quantitative-research/)

> Quantitative research generates numerical data or data that can be converted into numbers for a statistical review . . . Quantitative data are most often collected in the form of a questionnaire or survey. The research process typically involves the development of questions as well as scales that are used to measure feelings, satisfaction and other important factors on a numerical level.

If the data provided by this survey allow the Prego brand to adjust its recipe so that it included a type of tomato that was "preferred by a majority of chefs in Italian restaurants" this could be an extremely valuable finding—one that could both improve its product and form the basis of a powerful advertising campaign.

Evaluative Research

If, on the other hand, we wanted to know whether our strategy for selecting tomatoes, growing tomatoes and canning them for use in our sauce "worked," we'd have to evaluate our product. There are a number of ways we could go about conducting such evaluative research.

One way might be to use a *qualitative-evaluative* approach in which we gather a group of chefs, or family members, or neighbors together for a sauce tasting. We might sit them at a large table and have them compare the sauce we made with our tomatoes to a sauce we made with other, more ordinary or randomly selected, tomatoes. There are a number of steps we would take to make sure our results were valid and "actionable." For this qualitative evaluation, we might decide not to let our panel know which sauce was made with which tomatoes. Or we might not even let our panel know that it was the tomatoes that were the ingredient we manipulated for our taste test. In any event, we'd ask them to share their opinions, and we'd take note of what they said.

On the other hand, we might evaluate the product we made with our special tomatoes by doing a *quantitative-evaluative* study, in this case, a large-scale mall intercept study in which we provide the sauce in a taste test to a sample of a few hundred shoppers who agree to complete a survey after they sample our product. Or we might send our special sauce to a random sample of chefs who would agree to complete an evaluation from which we could calculate statistically significant results. In these cases, our evaluative research—either qualitative or quantitative— would provide the basis for adjusting the recipe for a refined sauce. This, by definition, would have transformed our evaluation into what is, in effect, new formative research.

STEP 2—Monitoring, Insights and Measurement: What We Learn from Social Media

If you're still wondering whether diving into social media makes sense for your organization, start by listening to social media conversations around your brand, competitors and industry before you do anything else. Try googling your organization's name, or that of your favorite brand, followed by the word *sucks*. You might be shocked at what you find.

Even if you can't envision your organization making social media a major part of your business strategy, learning how to eavesdrop on public conversations that are going on in social media can be a powerful skill set that will help you better understand your customers and your prospects.

Listening in on public social media conversations can help you discover opportunities and uncover threats. It can help you develop new or revised products and services, and it can help you shape and reshape the messages your organization is sending out through its words and its products, services and interactions with the community.

If your organization is already set up and running in one or more of the popular social media networks like Facebook, Twitter or Pinterest, for example, you are already participating in public conversations that can be, and possibly are being, monitored by a variety of people. By learning how to use social media monitoring tools yourself, you should be able to develop more relevant, elegant, engaging and profitable content and programs, services, products and relationships.

If you are still in need of some motivation to begin listening in on social media conversations that are going on about your products or services, think of this: Consider the possibility that your customers or prospects, friends and critics and certainly your competitors are eavesdropping on the social media conversations that are going on about you and your brand right now. And then ask yourself this question: Can I really afford to wait any longer to get involved myself?

Three Key Areas of Listening in on Social Media Conversations

Different organizations have different reasons for listening to social media conversations, but at its core, all listening is supported by three separate, yet interconnected, activities:

1. **Monitoring:** Real-time monitoring of social media networks identifies issues, opportunities, challenges and threats to our brand and our reputation.
2. **Insights:** What we overhear in social media is analyzed for context and trends, then fed back into the appropriate point within the organization and, hopefully, translated into action.
3. **Measurement:** The ongoing measurement and analysis of the organization's activities helps to determine what programs are working and how budgets and efforts can be reallocated to improve the impact of our marketing, content, business processes and products.

Each activity plays a different role but is a necessary condition of a social media monitoring effort that delivers real impact.

Monitoring Social Media: Well Begun is Half Done

To begin with, social media conversation monitoring is like an insurance policy for brands and organizations. You just never know when something is going to blow up in your face online and cause outrage among your customers, potential customers, employees, community groups or other stakeholders upon whom your organization depends for success and survival.

The last thing a brand needs is to be the target of a social media attack. What's even worse is when the organization isn't conscious of the attack happening until it's too late— until the attack has taken on a "social life" of its own. Especially in this day when social media play such a big role in the brands and reputation of any organization, a manager needs assurance that someone in the organization is keeping a regular ear to the ground of the social networks in order to make sure the organization can respond quickly and avoid being the lead story on tomorrow's morning shows for all the wrong reasons.

Obviously, just as the social networks have developed and grown, and with them the opportunities for social media crises, so has grown the list of great tools that are available to you. You can use these tools to reassure yourself and your organization's other leaders that there is no reason to lose sleep.

If the business is operating in an ethical manner in the interests of its customers, and you have an active social-conversation monitoring effort underway, you'll know immediately if anyone says something to the contrary. Fast action can correct bad chatter. If, on the other hand, your business is doing the wrong thing, somebody out there is talking about it, and picking up the chatter in social media may be the first way you and your team learns what's going on.

In future chapters, we'll walk you through these important steps:

- Finding the right listening tools.
- Creating a relevant list of keywords to monitor the social media chatter.
- Setting up real-time alerts around specific issues of interest to the business.
- Uncovering posts and trends that may require rapid response.
- Starting to get great business intelligence on perceptions and trends related to your organization, competitors and industry.
- Setting up a crisis action plan that can keep a small bonfire from becoming a firestorm.

These tools can help you become a key player on your organization's business intelligence team, crisis prevention and response team, marketing and market planning team and PR team. Here's how.

Spotting Opportunities for Creative New Products, Services and Marketing Activities

You don't have to look at monitoring social media conversations as a strictly defensive activity. There's much more to real-time monitoring and reporting than crisis prevention. There is no question that you can use the skills in this book to be well prepared to identify and respond to a business threat and quell a potentially damaging rumor. But let's focus on the positive. Imagine the role you can play in identifying and tracking positive industry trends, picking up on new product announcements, news or memes (an image, video, message, etc., being passed around on the Internet from one user to another) that you can tie into your own business initiatives.

And think about this: In the always-on world of social media, where all effective businesses understand that they are in the publishing business, organizations depend on marketers and public relations specialists to come up with frequent and relevant content. Once you learn how to keep an ear to the ground and eye on the trends, you will become a key player on the content team.

Taking advantage of this type of analysis is covered in Chapters 5 through 9.

Becoming a Customer Service Champion for Your Organization

Consumers have a new weapon in the arsenal to get their way with business or, if they don't get their way, to get even. Every day, more customers use social media to blast questions, concerns and complaints across the social media platforms they use. Fewer dissatisfied customers are picking up the phone or writing letters to company service departments; more and more are turning to social platforms to vent.

Customer complaints that have gone viral include everything from product quality issues to trouble assembling or using a product to complaints about discontinued or updated products. For brick and mortar retail stores, restaurants or other businesses, online complaints range from the quality and timeliness of products and services to the cleanliness or friendliness of the staff. Where a customer may have talked to a manager or left a comment card or called your corporate customer service line in the past, many now choose to blast away online in their preferred social networks.

Disgruntled consumers will work hard to make sure their complaints can be heard, but many don't expect to hear back. Many people are still shocked when they get a direct response from a company representative who wants to fix a problem that he first heard about in social media. For this reason, companies that respond to complaints quickly and honestly have an upper hand in the battle to get and keep customer loyalty. Think about it—it's easy to complain about someone behind his back, but it's disarming when you are approached by a company that knows you're unhappy, is hearing what you have to say and takes actions to make you happy.

A number of tricks of the trade for monitoring social media

networks for customer service issues are covered in Chapters 4, 5, 6 and 9.

Developing Insights Based on Market Intelligence to Improve Practices, Programs, Products and Services

We're in a new age of consumer research. From secure brand communities to the open online conversations, the way we seek out consumer insights has changed drastically. Social media conversation analysis is a little like an open focus group. More marketers are starting to see direct returns from uncovering insights from opinions that are already being expressed online in addition to (or instead of) asking direct questions through surveys, consumer interviews and focus groups.

Online conversation analysis offers the ability to gain an immediate understanding of how consumers are reacting to an organization, brand or general category. This understanding might influence anything from whether an advertisement continues to run to whether the ingredients or design of a particular product need to be reevaluated to make improvements.

Social media conversation analysis is discussed in Chapter 6, and you'll be diving in to find insights of your own in no time.

Keeping an Eye on Competitive Initiatives and Perceptions

Beyond understanding what people are saying about your brand, social media analysis can give you the ability to gain a deeper understanding of how people feel about your competitors. What is it that your competition is doing that people like? What are they doing that people don't like? What are your competitors' blind spots or points of vulnerability or gaps where your organization could fill a void? What other opportunities and threats should you be aware of as you plan your own products and advertising programming? The insights you get from social media analysis are beyond your current ability to imagine. Chapter 6 gives you the information you need to become a competitive research super sleuth.

Figuring Out Who Is Influencing the Social Conversations That Affect Your Brand and Your Marketing

Social media have opened a gate to allow anyone with enough creativity and commitment to become incredibly influential in any given niche. The line between blogging and mainstream journalism has blurred. Major blogs that have sprung up in the last decade have become primary sources of news for a growing number of people. In many cases, mainstream news outlets have been forced to develop their own online outlets, or they have purchased popular blogs to add to their media properties.

Technology news blogs help small start-ups gain traction. A do-it-yourself home improvement blogger has a passionate following that makes him a powerful force in the business life of Lowe's and Home Depot. A popular fashion blogger or Pinterest user may drive significant sales to featured fashion sites.

These new influencers are important to your organization on multiple fronts, and the time to start building relationships with them is now. Imagine how much easier it will be to manage new opportunities or respond to potential threats when you have relationships with a network of people who influence your industry.

You'll learn how to find the influencers who matter to you in Chapter 7.

Using Measurement Tools to Aim Resources at Targets That Matter

Measurement is like personal fitness. It's not something that you do just once—it's ongoing. You should be checking in on the health of your brand and competitors on an ongoing basis, just as you might step on a scale each day to see how much weight you've lost since your New Year's resolution began.

You can measure your brand's health in social media to better understand which of your products and programs are gaining traction, and which are not. With this understanding, you'll help your marketing or public relations teams tweak programs to put more focus (and budget) on what's working and to ignore or drop programs that are not. We not only measure conversations in social media, we also use our measurement tools to get a better understanding of the impact of our product launches, our advertising campaigns and other important activities.

Checking in on the social health of your organization and presenting your findings are covered in Chapters 5, 6, 8 and 9.

Gaining Feedback on Advertising to Improve Media Buys and Assist in Message Development

Social media doesn't happen in a vacuum. For many of the brands we've worked with, traditional advertising has been one of the largest drivers of social media conversation. People love to talk about advertising, and imbedded in their chatter are a variety of themes and specific messages that can be helpful across the organization.

In the same way that you can use social media analysis to track reactions to social programming, you can turn to social trends to determine how more traditional activity like your paid media is being perceived.

You'll read more on this in Chapters 5 and 6.

So, What Are You Waiting For?

Get ready to jump in and get started for yourself.

Chapter 3 takes a closer look at your own listening objectives to make sure you're getting the most out of listening.

❊ ❊ ❊

Making Your Practice Perfect

Exercise: What Can Social Media Tell You about a Brand?

Action 1: Google any major national soft drink brand name followed by the word *sucks*.

Action 2: Review at least the first 10 pages of comments (100 entries) and summarize in 100 words or less, and in general terms, what you find.

Action 3: Cluster the comments you find into three or four (at most) general categories of issues or complaints.

Action 4: Summarize (again in fewer than 100 words) what you could describe as the biggest threat facing the brand based on this very basic manual Google search.

Action 5: Identify any specific customer service actions you might take as a result of what you have found.

3

Setting Objectives for Social Media Listening

Without goals, and plans to reach them, you are like a ship that has set sail with no destination.

—Fitzhugh Dodson
Psychologist

In this chapter, you will learn:

- How to use our *"ID2 Approach"* for building a strong social media monitoring and measurement program.
- How to identify relevant team members.
- How to develop your business objectives for listening (reasons).
- How to investigate other data points that the team already has.
- How to decide who will do the listening and delegate.

Essential Term for Chapter 3

- Objective: An intended outcome, often thought of as the goal.

STEP 3—Setting Objectives for Social Media Listening

Getting Started

As the line between marketing and PR continues to blur, it's important that we recognize how different the two functions are. One reason for this is that as social media have gained traction, many marketers have struggled to figure out who "owns" the social media space within their organizations.

As you've seen, social media have come to influence everything from product development and customer service to decisions in paid and earned media and to the widest possible variety of relationships with the widest possible variety of an organization's stakeholders. Given the degree to which social media platforms and networks are becoming imbedded within virtually every aspect of an effective organization, this question of "ownership" begins to seem increasingly irrelevant. It's a little like asking: "Who in the organization owns the telephone?"

No matter who is executing social media monitoring and analysis for your organization, the information and insights from listening will be essential to, and must be immediately accessible to, everyone from the sales and marketing department to those more broadly concerned with building and maintaining organizational-public relationships.

To get things started, we are going to introduce you to five organizations with distinct business and listening objectives. These five organizations are going to be your "clients" as you learn to use tools to strengthen their positions in the marketplace, while enhancing your value as an important player on the team. You'll use these new skills to provide insights that directly affect your clients' profit or social impact. The organizations fall into the following categories:

- Small/local business and online retailer.
- National privately owned company.
- National restaurant chain.
- Nonprofit organization.
- Service-based consultancy (personal brand).

Mary: Eco Redux Studio
Category: Small/Local Business and Online Retailer

Mary runs a clothing boutique in Washington, DC, called Eco Redux Studio. All of the products she sources for the studio are eco-friendly.

Mary recently launched a new e-commerce website to help sell her clothing both online and in her boutique. She has never tried to connect with her in-store or online customers or prospects through social media networks.

Mary's freelance web developer is a woman named Lilly. Lilly has recommended that Mary get active in social media as a way of promoting the new online shop, but Mary doesn't know where to start. She does know that eco-fashion trends change quickly, and she would like to keep an eye on what topics and trends people who value eco fashion care about so that she can project demands and start engaging in more environment-related conversations with her customers and potential customers.

Maggie: Friendlie National Bank
Category: National Privately Owned Company

Maggie is a marketing manager for Friendlie National Bank. She and her team have taken steps to set up a professional social media listening tool with some basic keywords related to the company, but they feel overwhelmed by the number of ongoing social media conversations taking place about the bank and its competitors. They know people are asking questions and making comments about the bank, but they haven't yet set up a system to make sense of all of social media posts or to take action to respond to customer questions and complaints.

Tom: Mega Burger
Category: National Restaurant Chain

Mega Burger is a national restaurant chain. The company's director of digital marketing, Tom, has approached his PR agency, Covie PR, looking for innovative new ways to get people talking positively about Mega Burger.

Tom would like to use social media to build consumer awareness and positive sentiment around the restaurant chain. He has asked Dexter, Mega Burger's account manager at Covie PR, to present some ideas that include both creative plans and a way to measure the success of the proposed program.

Tom's team recently noticed what seems like a shift in customer complaints away from comment cards and phone calls and into social media. He's worried that what once was a private process between the complaining customer and the chain has now become a very public conversation about any little complaint. He feels that Mega Burger needs to develop a response program for these complaints. He has asked Covie PR to dig deeper into what is being said about Mega Burger in social networks, and to present their findings to the corporate customer service team as the first step in creating a plan of action.

Steven: Hartlin Kids

Category: Nonprofit Organization

Steven runs the communication team for Hartlin Kids, a nonprofit organization that delivers fresh fruit to underprivileged schools and promotes healthy eating and exercise for children across the state of Michigan.

Steven is most interested in using social media to bring attention to his cause, to increase donations and to further engage parents in the program. He knows that he needs to figure out what people are already saying about his organization and the issues that it addresses, especially about the availability of fresh fruits and vegetables to children. Steven is also interested in closely tracking any federal or state legislative issues related to childhood health, obesity and nutrition.

Steven's four-person communications staff has built relationships with most major newspapers and local television networks across their key regions in Michigan, and they send out a monthly email newsletter to their volunteers, donors, teachers, parents and selected traditional news media across the state. They have not considered listening to conversations in social media until now.

Amy: Marketing Consultant

Category: Service-based Consultancy (Personal Brand)

Amy is an independent marketing consultant working for small businesses in Chicago. Her current clients come from referrals from friends and other clients, but she would like to build her business by establishing herself as a marketing expert. To do this, she knows that she'll have to create more digital content and do more public speaking to small business groups. She's struggling to figure out where to start.

Four Actions for Building a Great Social Media Listening Program: The ID2 Approach (Identify–Develop–Investigate–Delegate)

Action 1: Identify All Relevant Team Members

Start your social media listening program by identifying individuals from around your organization who will benefit from having a strong social media listening program. This will likely include team members from:

- Operations
- Customer Service
- Product Development
- Public Relations, including external and internal communications
- Human Resources
- Marketing, including Advertising and Branding
- Sales
- Website Management
- Outside consultants in marketing, advertising, media buying, information technology and organizational-public relations.

Action 2: Develop Your Business Objectives for Listening (Reasons to Listen)

Let's say you're at a cocktail party or networking event and see a group of people talking in a circle. What do you do? Do you jump right in and start sharing your own stories with the group before getting to know who they are? No. You start by getting a feel for who the people are and what they care about, and then you offer up relevant conversational topics and stories for that particular group. Social media works the same way.

Your specific objectives for listening may fit into one or more of the categories listed below. Use this guide as a checklist to determine which objectives to focus on for your listening program.

A. Monitoring: Listen for Ongoing Threats and Opportunities

Respond to customer service issues:

—What complaints about our products or services are being discussed in social media?

—What questions do our customers or potential customers have that we could assist with?

—What social media platforms are our customers using to voice concerns?

—How does the volume of complaints or questions in social media compare to the volume of complaints or questions through other outlets (phone, email, comment cards, etc.)?

—Based on the volume of complaints and questions, how should we dedicate staff to handle customer service issues surfacing in social media compared to other outlets?

Keep an eye out for a potential crisis:

—Beyond day-to-day customer service complaints and questions, are there any product or service areas that could be potential threats to our organization's reputation (for example: product defects, sensitive business areas such as environmental or labor issues, ties to specific spokespeople or leadership or specific marketing initiatives)?

Spot opportunities for creative initiatives:

—What segment of the social media community is talking about our industry today? How can we engage with these social media outlets and individuals as new conversations are developing?

—Are we seeing any new trends related to our industry, or to the larger economy, that could be turned into a creative program or opportunity for our organization?

B. Insights: Using Marketing Intelligence to Improve Business Practices, Programs, Products and Services

Improve business practices and innovate on products and services by better understanding:

—Who are our customers? What do they care about? Can we use social listening to create customer personas, or representative "characters," that will help us better understand our core audiences?

—What do our customers like about our business and/or products?

—What do our customers dislike about our business and products/services?

Keep an eye on competitive initiatives and perceptions:

—What do people like about our competitors' products/services?

—What do people dislike about our competitors' products/services?

—What are social media conversations telling us about new business opportunities that would allow us to stand out from our competitors?

—What competitive advantages and disadvantages are being revealed by the social media conversations we examine?

Identify opportunities for new marketing initiatives:

—Are there topics or trends that people are discussing through social media that could drive our creative marketing initiatives or specific social content in a more effective direction?

—In which social media networks or niches are people talking about the topics that matter to our organization, and could we use this information to assist us in making media buys or seeking placement of content about our products or services?

Find out who is influencing social media conversations:

—Are there any specific outlets or individuals driving conversations in social media about our organization, industry or other topics that are relevant to us?

—How can we be proactive in building relationships with these influential outlets and individuals?

C. Measurement: Understand What's Working Well and What Isn't

Measure the results of specific programs in order to reallocate staff resources and budgets toward initiatives that are working:

—Which initiatives, products or services are resonating with our customers?

—Do we have any initiatives, products or services that are viewed negatively? If so, can we shift budget away from these negative areas and focus on areas that are producing more positive attention?

Gain feedback on traditional advertising in order to drive changes in future media buys or creative development:

—What advertising is resonating with our customers?

—Do we have any advertising that is offensive to people? What kind of people dislike our advertising and why?

—Do we have any old marketing materials (tag lines, promotions, advertising, etc.) that people still talk about positively? Can we continue to leverage these materials in any way?

Action 3: Investigate the Team's Other Existing Data Points

While social media trends and perceptions are powerful, they do contain a certain amount of bias based on who is most likely to express opinions online. This bias can create a distortion that might cause us to abandon strategies that are otherwise working effectively, or to continue to expand strategies that, in reality, are appealing only to the segment of our market that is heavily engaged in social media.

Think about the segments within your key stakeholder groups, including prospects, and ask yourself which of the popular social networking sites they are most likely to be using. Consider this:

> More than two-thirds of American adult Internet users are now connected to one or more social media platforms according to the most recent Pew Research Center's Internet and American Life Project (November 14-December 09, 2012).
>
> Facebook remains the most popular social networking site, with 67% of adult social media users engaged. It is especially appealing to adults between the ages of 18 and 29 (86%) and women (72%). Among adults 65 and older, slightly more than one-third of them are Facebook users.
>
> Twitter (16%), Pinterest (15%) and Instagram (13%) are the social networks of choice by a growing segment of the US adult Internet-using population. Adults ages 18-29 and African-Americans are the highest demographic sectors favoring the micro-blog Twitter. Women and adults under 50 with some college education constitute the largest Pinterest sector. Among Instagram fans, the

dominant sectors include young adults, African-Americans and Latinos.

Determine what data you are already collecting that could potentially be overlaid or that could work in tandem with the social media data points you have or will collect along the way. Examples include, but are not limited to:

—Sales data.
—Survey data (Do your customer service or other survey results align with social media perceptions?)
—Website analytics.
—Traditional media usage data.
—Focus group data.
—Traditional customer service data (How many people have called, emailed or written letters? Compare this data to social media questions and complaints. How do topics and sentiment vary across the different mediums?)

Action 4: Decide Who Will Do the Listening and Delegate

The specific listening objectives that your group develops will drive how your listening program gets staffed. A small organization may have a single individual or a small, dedicated team that manages all social media listening objectives. A larger organization may split varied objectives across more focused teams.

You will have to do some initial listening to gain a full appreciation of the context of existing social media conversations before you can make a final recommendation about how the social media monitoring will be allocated among the members of your team. We'll show you more details about how the listening actually occurs in the coming chapters.

Listening to social media and making the most of findings to take appropriate action may require cultural shifts within the organization. Consider the following questions when you meet as a team to discuss your listening objectives:

—Do we have the full support of the organizational leadership to focus some of our collective energy toward social media monitoring and measurement? If so, how does this support get conveyed to the team? If not, how do we go about getting the support we need to be successful?
—Who will execute initial social media listening? Who will

listen on a daily basis? Who will do the deeper dive analyses to understand larger trends?

—Should we designate an internal team to manage monitoring and analysis, or should we recommend bringing in an outside firm to help?

—How will responsibilities and budget be split among brand teams, corporate teams, customer service and/or insights teams?

—How will findings be reported back to the rest of the team, and then to the management of the organization?

—What other data do we have that can be examined side-by-side with our social media findings?

—Who should meet on a regular basis to discuss findings and recommend action based on our social media research?

—Will the results of online analysis be tied into advertising creative or media buying decisions through our advertising team?

—Will our customer service team need to be linked more closely with our PR team?

—For ongoing monitoring, will we monitor outside of business hours? Who will take charge if an issue arises outside of business hours?

—How do we plug our social media monitoring process into our organization's overall crisis prevention and crisis communication plan?

Ease Your Way into Listening

Don't try to take on all of these listening issues at once. Determine the objectives that matter most to your organization, and start there. You can revisit and adjust priorities later.

The ID2 Approach
(Identify–Develop–Investigate–Delegate)
for Our Five Organizations

Eco Redux Studio

1. Identify all relevant team members: Mary has three people on her staff. One team member, Sarah, is in charge of the new e-commerce site. She works with the company's freelance web developer, Lilly. Another team member, Martha, helps to manage public relations outreach to promote special events and seasonal collections at Eco Redux Studio with the local community in Washington, DC. Mary's third team member, Ellen, helps Mary locate and buy new products for the boutique.

Because Mary has a small team, she gathers all three of her teammates, along with Lilly.

2. Develop your business objectives for listening: The team sits down and lists top priorities for social media listening over the next three months:

—"We will improve products based on ongoing fashion trends." Mary knows that fashion trends change quickly, and she wants to stay on top of the most popular fashion trends and projections through social media to make sure her own projections align with trends in popular culture.

—"We will understand how people talk about Eco Redux Studio and sustainable products in order to create ideal customer personas that will direct our social content and marketing initiatives to push customers to the new e-commerce site." Mary hasn't created any social content yet. In order to make content messaging stronger and more targeted, Mary's team will evaluate social media conversations in order to better understand who their customers are and what they care about. They'll use this information to create customer personas—fictional characters that represent the attitudes, behaviors and demographics of their core audience—that will be used as an ongoing guide for new content.

—"We will understand where people talk about Eco Redux Studio and sustainable products in order to drive where we create social content and marketing initiatives to push customers to the new e-commerce site." Martha can help with content and marketing, but because her time is limited, she wants to be selective about where she sets up social media outlets for the boutique. Before putting any effort into setting up these social media outlets, she wants to learn which social media platforms hold the most opportunity around fashion and sustainable products.

—"We will determine which outlets or individuals are driving conversations in social media around eco-friendly fashion to build relationships that will help drive awareness around

Eco Redux Studio."The team members know that there has been an increased interest in eco-friendly products over the past few years, but they have never done any research to determine who is driving conversations around this topic in social media. Now that the boutique will be expanding its market beyond the local Washington, DC, area through its e-commerce store, Mary would like to find out who drives these conversations in order to build relationships for future initiatives.

—"We will improve customer service by connecting to customers online."Mary currently receives customer service inquiries via email and phone. She doesn't know whether customers are asking questions about her brand online, but she would like to find out where customers voice questions and concerns so that the team can be prepared to respond.

3. Investigate other data points that the team already has: Mary will work with Lilly and Sarah to cross-check social media findings with website analytics and sales data. This will help determine the best social media platforms for Eco Redux to focus on. Once the team understands the best platforms to engage in social media, they will continue to compare which platforms and types of content drive the most sales through the e-commerce site.

4. Delegate the individual (s) who will do the listening: Martha will kick off social media listening and content development. Long term, the team will evaluate whether it makes sense to set up a tablet in the boutique to have the staff track customer service issues as they happen.

Friendlie National Bank

1. Identify all relevant team members: Maggie's team works with a variety of specialty agencies. They have an advertising agency that produces their television, online, outdoor and print advertising material. The ads are purchased through a media-buying agency. The bank's public relations firm also participates with both agencies at several stages in the process, in part, in order to insure that the ads don't inadvertently disrupt relationships with the bank's different stakeholder groups. Friendlie Bank has an internal team that manages the website, along with a small internal team that recently set up a simple program to track and report basic customer complaints and to examine questions that customers ask through social media.

Maggie gathers a task force with representatives from each agency, along with the internal team that has already set up the basic listening program. Beyond this, she invites key product managers and brand managers, the director of sales and the head of customer service from her internal team to join the task force and sit down to discuss listening objectives.

2. Develop your business objectives for listening: The team sits down and lists top priorities for social media listening over the next three months. Here they are:

—"We will understand trends involving both customer complaints and compliments so that this information can be used to improve ongoing service and products, and be used to develop new ones."The internal listening team knows that complaints and compliments are being posted through social media each day, but they have never analyzed which issues are driving the most discussion in social media. Once the team has determined top drivers of both negative and positive social media conversations around specific products and services, they will cross-check this information with quarterly survey results and reports of in-person focus groups in order to prioritize the areas that should be adjusted and updated within the organization.

—"We will improve customer service by connecting to customers online."Friendlie Bank's team already tracks customer service issues. Now they want to analyze trends around the types of issues that are being discussed in order to set up a team response plan that is aimed at improving customer service.

—"We will understand what our competitors are doing so that information can be fed into our product development unit and can be reflected in our marketing and public relations messages."Friendlie Bank has never listened in on the public social media conversations about its competitors. The team has decided to track public conversations about four targeted competitors. The data this effort uncovers will complement the research related to Friendlie Bank's complaints and its compliments to help drive future products and services as well as marketing and public relations initiatives.

—"We will systematically listen for ongoing threats and opportunities." Beyond individual customer service responses, the team, especially the head of public relations, is concerned about emerging issues that have the potential to affect the organization's overall reputation. The team wants to put a plan in place to track larger trends and potential threats in order to respond quickly. They want to make sure that there is a clear and direct line between the potential reputational threats discovered in social media and the organization's overall crisis prevention and communication plan. They also want to identify opportunities that emerge in social media that can be used to tell a positive story about Friendlie Bank on an ongoing basis.

—"We will advocate for the reallocation of resources and business expenses toward those initiatives that we determine are gaining the most positive results."Friendlie Bank's advertising and public relations agencies agree that listening to conversations in social media will be useful to develop and push creative initiatives and media buys. The team will advocate for those initiatives that people respond most positively to in social media. By determining where people are talking and what they are talking about, the team hopes to drive more targeted media buys for Friendlie Bank as well.

3. Investigate other data points that the team already has: Friendlie Bank already conducts quarterly customer surveys that reveal customer sentiment around specific products and bank services. These data points will be compared to social media findings in order to facilitate decisions around product and service updates. The team will also use in-person focus groups to test new ideas around product updates. Friendie Bank also plans to overlay phone and email customer service complaints with social media complaints to determine which areas drive the most complaints and prioritize updates.

4. Delegate the individual(s) who will do the listening: Maggie's internal listening team will continue to execute the social media research and monitoring based on the objectives determined by the agency task force. From there, the internal team will meet monthly with the agency task force to make sure findings are being communicated across agencies and units of the organization on an ongoing basis. As the listening team gains a better understanding around the volume and context of specific customer service requests, they will work closely with the customer service unit to put a response plan in place over the next 90 days.

Mega Burger

1. Identify all relevant team members: Tom's team already has a monthly status meeting with the larger marketing staff at Mega Burger. They have not worked directly with the customer service team regarding social media listening up to this point. Tom asks Dexter's team at Covie PR to join the next status meeting to discuss objectives for listening. He also invites Mega Burger's head chef, the head of customer service and a few local store managers to join the conversation.

2. Develop your business objectives for listening: The team sits down and lists top priorities for social media listening over the next three months:

— "We will evaluate reactions to specific menu items to support future menu development." The Mega Burger team decides to research reactions to specific menu items through social media. This information will be cross-referenced with sales data to drive future menu changes. The team will also track trends and context around what people specifically like and dislike about menu items in order to create new product variations for the future.

— "We will understand the perception of our competitors in order to assist in the development of marketing messages and product innovation." The team decides to listen to social media conversations from three targeted competitors to gain a better understanding of what marketing initiatives they have in place and how people are reacting to their messaging. The team also wants to understand what people like and dislike about specific menu items at each competitor to assist in data-driven decision making for revised or new products, pricing and presentation in menus.

— "We will help improve customer service by connecting

directly to customers online." Mega Burger's customer service team tracks and follows up with complaints from patrons at the restaurant, along with in-restaurant comment cards, phone calls and emails. The social media monitoring team will incorporate social media listening into this tracking and determine how to involve customer service staff more directly in the social listening program.

—"We will listen for ongoing threats and opportunities."Dexter recommends that Mega Burger keep an eye out for larger potential issues that may affect the brand's reputation, along with watching ongoing day-to-day trends and influencers in social media that may present opportunities for the brand to share positive stories. Given the consumer-orientation of the products and recent industry examples of social media disasters that have gone viral, the team will ensure that they can provide "real-time" information to the public relations leader in order to prevent or mitigate attacks or errors that have the capability to go viral.

—"We will identify topics and trends that people are discussing through social media that could potentially drive creative marketing initiatives or specific social content."Dexter recommends that his team do ongoing research on broader trends in social media related to food and restaurants to determine what type of social media content is most likely to resonate with current and potential customers and which social platforms the team should be focusing on.

—"We will determine which outlets or individuals are driving conversations in social media around Mega Burger and the broader food and restaurant categories to build relationships for future initiatives." Along with topics and trends, Dexter proposes that his team research specific outlets and individuals who are driving conversations related to Mega Burger specifically, and the food and restaurant industry in general, in order to build relationships for the future. This will tie directly to social content and ongoing initiatives.

—"We will make recommendations for the reallocation of resources, including business expenses, by focusing on initiatives that gain the most positive results." Tom asks Dexter to come up with a plan to track reactions to Covie PR's ongoing initiatives and report the findings back to his team at Mega Burger in order to recommend changes and focus efforts on areas that are driving the most positive results in social media.

3. Investigate other data points that the team already has: Mega Burger plans to start by comparing phone and email customer service complaints with social media complaints to determine which areas of the current business drive the most complaints. The company also plans to overlay sales data related to specific products against these data points in order to aid in decision making around menu development.

4. Delegate the individual (s) who will do the listening: Tom's team is small and focused. Because of this, he asks Dexter's team to do the initial social media listening research for Mega Burger. The Covie PR team will be a part of the ongoing monthly status meetings with the full team, and specific findings will be distributed to the head chef and head of customer service on an ongoing basis.

Hartlin Kids

1. Identify all relevant team members: Steven sets up a meeting with his immediate team, along with Hartlin Kids' director, Sheila, and the director of fundraising, Matt.

2. Develop your business objectives for listening: The team sits down and lists top priorities for social media listening over the next three months:

- —"We will track legislative issues and trends related to childhood health, obesity and nutrition."Steven wants to make sure his team stays on top of new legislative issues related to Hartlin Kids' mission so that he can be prepared to communicate and respond to these issues as needed.
- —"We will identify national topics and trends that people are discussing through social media that could influence our creative marketing initiatives or our specific social content and are capable of increasing issue awareness and donations for Hartlin Kids." Beyond legislative issues, Steven wants his team to be aware of other topics and trends that may be used to drive social content for Hartlin Kids. At this point, Steven's team does not yet have a presence in any

social media platforms. He would like to determine which platforms and types of content will be the best fit to communicate with key audiences: existing and potential volunteers, donors, teachers and parents.

—"We will determine which specific outlets or individuals are driving conversations in social media around topics related to childhood health, nutrition and exercise in order to start building relationships with them."Steven wants to expand his team's relationships into the social space. He wants to learn who is influencing discussions on topics that matter to Hartlin Kids in social media so that his team can start building relationships with appropriate outlets and individuals in the social space.

—"We will recommend the reallocation of the team's time to focus on initiatives that gain positive results." As Steven's team begins to get involved with social media, he wants to make sure they are tracking both online and offline initiatives to find out what is leading to the most positive responses around volunteer engagement and sign up, donations and involvement from teachers and parents.

3. Investigate other data points that the team already has: Steven will compare offline and online volunteer sign-up forms and donation forms that show where current supporters have heard and are hearing about the work of Hartlin Kids.

4. Delegate the individual (s) who will do the listening: Steven assigns initial listening setup and analysis to two members of his communications team. He will work closely with them to guide the project.

Amy, Independent Marketing Consultant

1. Identify all relevant team members: As a solo marketing consultant, Amy will be doing her own listening.

2. Develop your business objectives for listening: Amy sits down to brainstorm top priorities for social media listening over the next three months:

—"I will identify topics and trends related to small business marketing that people are discussing through social media to drive expert content to build credibility."Before Amy puts a content plan in place, she wants to take some time to understand what others talk about related to small business marketing so that she can find her own unique angle to stand out with her own content and personal brand.

—"I will identify upcoming conferences and speaking opportunities."Amy would like to set up a system to track local events and upcoming conferences to begin to identify events where she can network or speak.

—"I will track popular blogs related to small business marketing in order to start engaging and building relationships for future guest posts."Amy would like to start tracking specific blog posts that mention topics related to small business marketing so that she can engage with the authors, build a relationship and reach out for future guest posts or expert interviews.

3. Investigate other data points that the team already has: Amy currently has some information, much of which is anecdotal, regarding how she has acquired contacts that have led to client engagements. She'll review each client she has acquired in the recent past and create an index of the characteristics of previous client acquisitions.

4. Delegate the individual (s) who will do the listening: Amy will start by setting aside time in her schedule to track conversations, engage with relevant blogs and write content each morning.

Next Steps: Determine Where to Listen

Now that you know why you want to listen, it's time to determine where to listen. We'll select a set of listening tools to track and analyze the media types that tie back to your listening objectives.

—Facebook (including both public Facebook posts and brand pages)
—Twitter
—Blogs
—Blog comments
—Forums
—Photo sharing (e.g., Flickr or Twitter photos such as Instagram, Twitpic, yfrog, Lockerz or others)
—Videos

—Mainstream media
—Pinterest
—Tumblr
—Podcasts

Some of the media types listed above are easier to track than others. Next, we'll select a set of listening tools to track and analyze the ones that tie back to your listening objectives.

* * *

Making Your Practice Perfect

Exercise: Setting Your Listening Objectives

It's time to take action. Use the ID2 model to outline the details and objectives of your own listening plan for the next 90 days:

—Identify all relevant team members.
—Develop your business objectives for listening.
—Investigate other data points that your team already has.
—Delegate the individual(s) who will do the listening.

4

Selecting the Best Social Media Monitoring Tools for Your Organization

---

We all have non-negotiable relationships and outfits
we adore that we can't possibly throw away.
But we also all have things in our life
we want to eliminate and audit out.

—Caroline Righton
Author
The Life Audit

In this chapter, you will learn:

- How to set a list of non-negotiables to be used to select appropriate listening tools.
- How to establish criteria for evaluating listening tools.
- How to evaluate key features of listening tools.

Essential Terms for Chapter 4

- **Automated Analysis:** Machine-driven analysis of social media sentiment and context.
- **Data Portability:** The ability to move data from one application or computing environment to another (e.g., CSV export).

- **Non-Negotiables:** A list of *must-have factors* or *features*. Within the context of this book, non-negotiables are used to describe those must-have features within social media listening tools an individual selects. Examples of these features might be price range or types of media covered by the tool.

STEP 4—Selecting the Best Social Media Monitoring Tools for Your Organization

In today's media monitoring landscape, it feels like new listening tools are being launched every week. Each tool claims to be the best at something, but the truth is that there is no single perfect tool that can do everything we'd like to be done perfectly. There is no set standard for what features a tool should offer, and there's no precise list of social media elements that communications professionals should be monitoring or measuring. So, it's important to set up a clear checklist of conditions you want to see met when you're getting ready to select the right listening tools for your goals.

Know that as you find gaps in tools—things you want done that your selected tool can't handle—you will have to select other free or paid tools to fill those gaps. This is especially true as new popular social platforms arrive on the scene. No social monitoring tool provider, for example, could have possibly anticipated that Pinterest or Instagram would have the large and almost immediate impacts that they had in social media culture. The tools to measure the impact of these platforms had to be developed well after these new networks made the scene.

Remember, there are some basic social media monitoring tools that are available to you at no charge. We'll look at these later. But let's begin our selection process by coming up with a set of factors that can be used as you evaluate the "paid-for" social media monitoring and analysis tools.

An exercise at the end of this chapter asks you to select an appropriate set of tools based on your own evaluation.

Buying Factors

Factors to evaluate before buying social media-monitoring tools include:

- Pricing structure
- Media-type coverage

- Access to historical data
- Data portability
- Usability
- Integration with social accounts
- Languages
- Customer service
- Special features

Pricing Structure

Here's the first thing you should know: There is no standard for how monitoring and measurement tool providers structure the pricing for their tools.

We met with one business owner who joked that it felt like evaluating the pricing of these tools was like throwing darts at a dartboard. Prices for monitoring tools are all over the map. Prices range from a few dollars per month to six figures per year, and they are changing all the time.

Most providers of tools base their pricing on some combination of the following factors:

- Number of social posts returned from your keyword searches (monthly post volume).
- Number of keyword search terms.
- Number of topics. For example, some tools will allow you to break out keyword sets by topic, which may include specific marketing keywords, products, alerts, competitors, etc.
- Number of users.
- Access to historical data. Some tools will add an up-charge to get access to older social media posts.
- Media (or social network) types monitored, such as Facebook, Twitter, blogs, forums, etc.
- Integration with social profiles (e.g., Twitter, Facebook).
- Additional special features.

Is Pricing Based on the Volume of Social Posts?

We've seen the volume of social media posts increase by 5 to 15 times across brands that we've tracked just over the past three years. This increase results from a combination of factors:

—The tools are getting better at pulling more data, such as

the inclusion of public Facebook posts that weren't included a few years ago.

—General social media conversations have increased as more people adopt social media.

—Some brands have experienced additional growth from actively engaging and responding with customers in social media.

If the right tool for you is one that bases its pricing on post volume, you need to be well aware of the potential for that volume to skyrocket over the next few years. If this seems likely, see if you can lock in a fixed price based on current volume that will remain in effect if your volume increases. This is especially important since many budgets are set at least a year in advance.

Is Pricing Based on a Set Number of Keywords or Topics?

Many tools have pricing structures that are based on how many search terms you're setting up rather than on the volume of social posts. This arrangement also has its limitations. For example, we have worked with many brands that track 20 or more specific initiatives at once.

Pricing based on the number of keywords can also be very limiting for those brands that are unfortunate enough to share a name with other common phrases, since this will often produce a large number of irrelevant posts, and it will require a greater number of keywords to refine results. Your team might have to decide what is more important for the organization's particular objectives—unlimited volume or unlimited searches.

We use a wide range of tools to accommodate the different clients with which we work. Each tool choice involves a number of tradeoffs.

Media-Type Coverage

Media-type coverage can get tricky, especially when it comes to Facebook. Many specialty tools cover only one media type, such as Boardreader.com for forums, Google Blog Search for blogs and a number of analytics tools focused solely on Twitter, Facebook and other social platforms.

Make a list of the media types that you know you want to cover based on your objectives. This list may include (but is not limited to):

—Twitter
—Blogs
—Blog comments
—Forums
—Photo sharing (e.g., Flickr or Twitter photos such as Instagram, Twitpic, yfrog, Lockerz or others)
—Facebook
—MySpace
—Videos
—Mainstream media
—Pinterest
—Facebook (both public Facebook posts and brand pages)
—Tumblr
—Podcasts

Along with specific media types, try out some sample searches to compare the volume and accuracy of search results across tools. For example, some free tools are described as having the capacity to monitor across most media types, but they only return a fraction of the actual social media posts in their search results. Others may show a higher volume of search results only because spam and bots drive a huge percentage of those posts.

The best way to determine whether a tool is returning quality results is to check it out by running a test using sample keyword searches.

Access to Historical Data

If you think that you may need to look back at previous social conversations for analysis and comparison, your tool options will be a bit more limited, and you'll likely pay a premium for that privilege. If you plan on pulling data from today forward, or 30 days back, you'll have more options, but be sure to find out how flexible these data become once you start looking back at previous months and years.

Our team once worked with a tool that only allowed us to pull social media posts from the time we entered our keywords, and we had no ability to go back to historical posts. It did the trick and pulled social conversations for us, but whenever we found keywords that were pulling in a lot of irrelevant posts, it was incredibly difficult and frustrating to go backward and filter those out to keep our data from being distorted when it came time to begin analysis.

For example, if we decided to filter out the words *coupon* or *coupons*, the tool would start filtering those out from the time we removed these words. However, we had to go back and manually remove all previous posts with those keywords in order to compare apples to apples across time. Believe us when we tell you that that was not fun. We ended up switching tools based on a reevaluation of our needs. Be sure to find out how flexible the tools are that you're evaluating.

Data Portability

Data portability is a big deal. It involves the ability to move data from one application or computing environment to another. Data portability will become an essential issue when we get into more detail around social media analysis in later chapters. And it's just one more reason why you have to think your whole process through before selecting your tool or tools. Think about these portability questions as you are evaluating each tool:

—Can you export social posts to what are called comma-separated value (CSV) files, or any other format, that you can easily edit using spreadsheet software?
—Can you export charts to include in your own reports?
—Can you set up email or RSS alerts to track keywords related to specific issues?

Usability

Usability is a more subjective issue than portability, and as a result, it's harder to judge. Usability usually takes significant forethought to truly understand, and it typically requires a demonstration or free trial to dive in and test the tool out.

Each tool is set up with a vastly different interface, so it's important to gauge, at least on a basic level, what the learning curve will look like to get you and your team members up to speed on the tool.

We've seen far too many cases where companies have signed contracts and invested thousands of dollars in tools before testing them. After the tools are delivered, they find that the tools are much too complicated for their personnel, and the learning curves are much too steep; as a result, the tools are not being used as intended.

Integration with Social Accounts

If your team plans to set up accounts on social platforms such as Twitter, Facebook, Pinterest or others, consider whether the tool you select will allow you to connect to these accounts to respond directly to issues and opportunities as they are spotted. This may make your daily workflow easier as you get more involved with monitoring and responding to social media posts.

Languages

Many tools are described as being able to monitor for, and sometimes translate to, multiple languages. Be aware that cultural differences in different regions go beyond the subtle and nuanced meaning of different languages.

The list of most popular social media platforms differs from country to country. Do your research into the region or country in which you are looking to monitor in order to make sure that you recognize these differences. You may find that you will need different tools to monitor the different social media platforms in use in different countries or regions.

Again, don't expect one single tool to cover all of your needs. Just as different brands will have different priorities, different regions and countries will have significant differences as well.

Customer Service

The last big factor we're dealing with is customer service. Again, you'll have to do a little detective work to figure this out, but you'll want to know that if the tools are not working as you hoped, you won't be left hanging. There's no substitute for a reference check; and for a decision as important as selecting the right tools for the job, there's no excuse for not checking references.

Do a little digging to find out who else is using the tool and talk with them to determine how happy or unhappy they are.

Find out whether you'll have a specific service representative who will handle your account. Check to see if you'll have a direct support phone number, email or Twitter handle to get an immediate response when you have questions or if the tool doesn't run the way you expect. You might even use some of your newly developed monitoring skills to see what current or former customers are saying about how well the provider has handled client issues or complaints in the past, and look at the tool provider's Twitter handle to see if the company is actively responding to questions

Additional Special Features

Of course, there could very well be other factors that you want to take into account based on your unique needs. Here are a few examples of special features:

—Ability to integrate the tool with your organization's social pages and handles to manage social posts and track engagement directly.

—Ability to sort posts by Twitter followers, views, comments, etc.

—Ability to set up email alerts to track specific topics.

—Ability to sort by "influence" (typically based on a proprietary formula).

—Geo-targeting (sort by country, region, etc.).

—Access to demographic or geographic information.

Evaluating the Right Listening Tools for Your Organization

Now that you know the major factors for making the right tool selection, it's time to dive in and start gathering information. But be aware: It's not always easy to find all of the information you need right on the provider's website, so let's walk through a few simple approaches for filling out this list:

—Begin by creating a spreadsheet—either a formal or "yellow pad" spreadsheet—that will allow you to compare all of your potential tools against the same criteria we identified in the list above.

—Go to each company's website to see what information it offers up publicly about the tool you are reviewing. Some companies offer more information than others do, of course.

—Do a search on *http://twitter.com/search* for the tool name to get an idea of how people feel about the tool and whether they have any complaints. This essentially turns conversation research in on itself to get a crowd-sourced view of what others think about the tool. The same goes for blogs and forums.

—Do a simple search on *Google.com/blogsearch* (blog search) or *Boardreader.com* (forum search) to find out if others have written reviews or opinions about the tools.

—Set up a free trial if the tool has one available. Set up an actual search and evaluate your experience with the tool.

—Set up a demonstration. Some tools will host regular webinars that will let you see a demonstration and ask questions. Others set up private demonstrations by request. You can usually set these up through the website. We always recommend the walk-through if it's available. This will give you a chance to ask questions.

—Talk to others. Every time we go to conferences or networking events and talk to others who are involved in social media monitoring and analysis, we learn something new about a new tool or feature that's worth keeping on our radar screen.

—Whether you're on Twitter, a forum, a blog or in person, ask for others' opinions.

Take it one step at a time. Don't try to review every tool out there—it's simply not possible. Start by comparing three to five tools that meet your basic needs and budget. You can always add more tools later if you choose.

There may still be some gaps in the information you are able to collect. You won't know everything you need to know until you use the tool, or you'll run into problems that you hadn't anticipated. This always happens, but do the best you can to inform yourself up front on these key issues. Have your objectives and your list of non-negotiables in front of you as you evaluate each tool.

Filling in the Gaps: Free Social Search and Analytics Tools

Professional listening tools will add power and sophistication to your monitoring and research, but no single tool will be able to provide everything you need in one single package. This means that you'll need basic knowledge about specialized tools to fill in some gaps.

The good news is that a huge number of free tools are at your fingertips. The bad news is that free tools are sometimes sold off to other companies or shut down for one reason or another, so if you use one of these, you have to be prepared to make a switch to another tool at a moment's notice.

Here are a few of our favorite free social media search and analysis tools based on usability and search results. This list is by no means comprehensive. You can find numerous additional tools and recommendations by doing a Google search for "free social media monitoring tools" or "free social media analytics tools."

Social Search and Monitoring

- Blinkx (http://blinkx.com): videos
- BoardOmgili (http://omgili.com): forums
- Flickr (http://flickr.com): photos
- Google Blog Search (http://google.com/blogsearch): blogs
- Google Video Search (http://google.com/videohp): video
- Ice Rocket (http://icerocket.com): blogs, Facebook, Twitter, images
- Kurrently (http://kurrently.com): Facebook and Twitter
- PinReach (http://pinreach.com): Pinterest
- Reachli file://localhost/(http://reachli.com): Pinterest
- Social Mention (http://socialmention.com): Twitter, blogs, comments, images, news, videos
- Statigram (http://statigr.am): Instagram
- Twilert (http://twlert.com): Twitter alerts
- Twitter Search (http://twitter.com/search): Twitter

Twitter Analytics

- BackTweets (http://backtweets.com)
- HootSuite (http://hootsuite.com)
- Twitter Counter (http://twittercounter.com)
- TwitSprout (http://twitsprout.com)
- TweetStats (http://tweetstats.com)
- Twitalyzer (http://twitalyzer.com)

Track Clicks

- Bitly (http://bitly.com)

- HootSuite (http://hootsuite.com)
- Twitpic (http://twitpic.com): track Twitter photo views

Website Analytics
- Compete (http://compete.com)
- Facebook Insights (available on your Facebook page)
- Google Analytics (http://google.com/analytics)
- Quantcast (http://quantcast.com)

Check out Ken Burbary's wiki (wiki.kenburbary.com) for another comprehensive list of both free and paid tools. He provides links directly to the tools' websites, along with basic details for each.

Another PR pro, Tracy Lewis, recently updated her own social media monitoring tools comparison guide (google "Social Media Monitoring Tools Comparison Guide"). She uses a slightly different set of criteria for selection than we do, but there is great overlap among all of the lists.

Human Versus the Machine: A Word on Automated Analysis

In a perfect world, everything could be accomplished by the touch of a button. Alas, this world is far from perfect, and it's far too complicated to rely on buttons alone. The world requires a human touch in order to have any chance of running smoothly, and so does social media monitoring and analysis.

If you're evaluating a tool and something seems too good to be true, it probably is. Be especially wary of any tool that claims to be able to automatically sort social media posts by sentiment, emotion or intent. While natural language processing (artificial intelligence and linguistics) tools have advanced greatly, as we said earlier, most tools still require human interaction to make sense of social conversation trends and determine full context or intent.

If you are watching a live demonstration of a tool and the sales representative claims automation of sentiment, emotion or intent, ask the representative how accurate the tool is, and ask to see the tool in action by looking at exact examples of posts that the tool pulls through.

Even if a technology claims to truly understand the English language, it is still difficult for it to understand sarcasm, misspellings or slang, all of which are prevalent across social media posts. To illustrate this point, take a look at the sample posts below. These posts were pulled through one automated tool as "negative" posts related to Netflix around the time that the company changed its subscription service. We didn't have to dig very deep to find these examples. All of these posts were found within the first 25 of more than 23,000 posts that were listed as negative:

> "@Netflix not sure what everyone is crying about. Thanks for all these years of great service."

> "Imagine if Netflix and Qwikster combined services . . . unlimited DVD rentals and streaming. Now THAT would be awesome."

> "Laying watching desperate housewives on Netflix."

Contrast that to the following posts we found that were listed as positive according to automated sentiment. Note words like "funny," "love" and "hilarious"—all words that may typically be associated with positive thoughts:

> "Dear Netflix, we're offering special prices & 30-day trials of Blockbuster Total Access to your members #helloBlockbuster"

> "Dear Netflix, *Phew* thanks for saving us from bankruptcy. Love, Blockbuster"

> "That letter from the Netflix owner was hilarious. Who is he kidding? Won't see part of my paycheck again"

Chapter 6 covers automated analysis versus human analysis in greater depth.

Callouts

Here's what some of the experts say about automated sentiment:

> Any analysis of sentiment (be it human or automated) comes with problems of accuracy and interpretation, but the bigger challenge to really

understand what is being said in social is that sentiment is often applied to a whole sentence or even to a whole post (Tweet, blog post. etc). Misinterpretation risks producing generalizations that are meaningless—in any given post multiple issues can be discussed and the author may express different opinions about each issue. For automated sentiment analysis tools to be really valuable they need to get better at understanding the semantics of any post and identifying the objects about which sentiment is actually being expressed. —Matt Rhodes, Director, Fresh Networks

Automated sentiment and analysis is still very crude and rudimentary. We are a long way from something that will be acceptable to professional corporate communicators. It can help you sift some raw data to try and reduce it down to a manageable level for human analysis, but even then you risk missing important stuff. My advice to clients is that if you really want to use these tools then you'll inevitably choose the 'least worst' rather the 'best.'—Stuart Bruce, Public Relations and Corporate Communications Trainer and Consultant

Automated sentiment analysis is at best 50% accurate. Language on social media is unstructured and filled with slang, double negatives and sarcasm—this skews any automated analysis. The only real way to get proper insight is a hybrid approach with humans looking at search results. —Giles Brown, Director, Social360

Sentiment analysis will never be 100% accurate. Even in tests involving two humans looking at the same statements, they only agree 80-85% of the time, on average. Therefore, a machine is clearly never going to be correct 100% of the time. Having said that, sentiment analysis has improved greatly, and continues to improve. Keyword dictionaries are, largely, not good enough . . . the Web is full of slang, sarcasm and nonsense.

We use a rules based system that is constantly audited and updated to account for emerging trends in language. The rules used to classify sentiment in our tool are written by, and unique to, us. They take into account much more than just the words used—for example, the ordering and placement of specific words within a statement. Of course, sarcasm will always be extremely difficult for a machine to detect, but that doesn't mean that automated sentiment analysis can't be useful. Even if not 100% accurate, automated analysis can be useful for giving a snapshot of sentiment and can alert you to possible issues. For example, if there is suddenly a huge increase in mentions being classified as negative, then chances are something is going on that you need to look into. I think as long as you are aware that sentiment analysis is never going to be perfect, it can be extremely useful.— Jasmine Jaume, Community Manager, Brandwatch

I'm very pragmatic about automated sentiment analysis. It's not a silver bullet, but it has its uses, especially when dealing with high-volume content. It's imperfect, and if you're going to depend on it, you need to test it first.

But I really think that we've put too much emphasis on sentiment analysis, regardless of the coding method. I'm more interested in the other things people do with this data, whether it's extracting topics and emotions or running it through analysis other than text analytics. The usual conflation of social media, text analytics, and customer opinion is interesting and useful, but it's not the only thing we might want to do with this data.

—Nathan Gilliatt, Principal, Social Target

Set Your Non-Negotiables

Write down a list of your basic "must haves"—the non-negotiables that these tools will help your brand or organization accomplish based on the listening objectives you put together in

Chapter 3. Next, prioritize other elements or features that would be nice to have.

Here are a few questions to consider:

—Are you operating on a fixed budget?

—Do you need a free tool (or tools)?

—Are there particular media types that you absolutely must be able to track? Is historical data important?

—Do you have a high level of conversation volume?

—How many competitors or topics do you want to be able to track?

—Do you want to be able to sort and find influencers?

—Do you want the tool(s) to integrate directly with your brand Twitter account?

Let's take a look at a few examples.

Eco Redux Studio

Because Mary is still determining which social platforms are the most relevant for her needs, she needs a tool that can track social media posts across multiple media types. She will look for a tool that does not structure pricing based on volume, since fashion tends to be a high-volume topic.

Ideally, the tool or tools she uses will integrate with the studio's own social accounts once the team starts creating content and getting more engaged with its customers.

If possible, Mary would like to find a tool that allows the team to sort posts based on engagement (e.g., Twitter followers, replies, retweets, blog comments, inbound links or shares) in order to discover daily opportunities for engagement and relationship building with influential outlets and social users.

As a small company, Mary would like to find a set of budget-friendly tools for less than $100 per month. She is willing to work with a less sophisticated tool in order to keep costs down.

Friendlie National Bank

Because social post volume around Friendlie Bank and competitors is high, Maggie's team needs a tool that will allow them to evaluate 500,000 to one million social posts in any given month.

The price of the tool should not be based on the number of

keyword searches in order to allow more flexibility for breaking out specific programs and products within the organization.

The tool will need to cover multiple media types and allow for deeper analysis of the data, along with the ability to export the data for further analysis and reporting by the team. It should allow the team to sort posts based on engagement (e.g., Twitter followers, replies, retweets, blog comments, inbound links or shares) in order to discover daily opportunities for engagement and relationship building with influential outlets and social users.

The team is willing to spend more to find a more sophisticated tool that will save time with monitoring and analysis.

Mega Burger

The team needs a tool that will allow them to evaluate a high volume of social media posts across multiple media types. It will have the ability to break out a high number of specific keywords and topics related to menu items, customer service and competitors. Ideally, it will integrate with Mega Burger's own social accounts to help the team track customer service issues and complaints.

Because the tool will be used to evaluate ongoing initiatives to make business decisions, the team is willing to spend more for a more sophisticated tool that will save time with monitoring and analysis.

Hartlin Kids

Steven's team is particularly interested in tracking Twitter, blogs and mainstream news for legislative issues and national trends that could be relevant to Hartlin Kids. Steven expects that he will find a fairly high level of social conversations around children's health, nutrition and childhood obesity, so he would like to find a tool that does not limit him based on post volume.

The tool should allow the team to sort posts based on engagement (e.g., Twitter followers, replies, retweets, blog comments, inbound links or shares) in order to discover daily opportunities for engagement and relationship building with influential outlets and social users.

Steven would like to find a tool that allows him to tag and sort social posts to understand which initiatives are gaining the most positive results.

Amy (Marketing Consultant)

Amy would like to find a low-cost or free set of tools to aggregate relevant social posts. Ideally, she would like to be able to track tweets by keyword and location to find people talking about events in her area. She would also like to track blogs and online mainstream news.

Amy is willing to sacrifice sophistication for a lower cost.

Next Steps: Set Up Search Keywords

Now that you know why you want to listen, where to listen and what tools you will use to listen, it's time to create a list of specific search keywords to track.

―――――――

CASE STUDY 4.1—Selecting Viralheat as the Tool of Choice for the Direct Marketing Educational Foundation (DMEF)—A report of a DMEF student intern

DMEF Mission Statement

To attract, educate and place college students in direct/interactive marketing careers. We are dedicated to engaging students in order to educate them about the direct and interactive marketing industry in addition to providing them with invaluable opportunities and funds to support their immersion in this industry.

Overall Goals for Social Media Use

The high school/college generation is often considered the age group to be most "digital-savvy"—they know how to use social media and love doing it. Because the mission of our organization is to predominately engage with college students in order to educate them about the industry, we realize there is no better place to do this than social communities. By using social media as a medium to communicate with this generation of future business leaders, it has been easier for them to access the information that is relevant to them, that we want them to see, and thus to engage with us.

Goals for Using Viralheat

I examined Viralheat based on the recommendation of Rand Schulman, who used to serve on the Viralheat board and was an incoming board member of DMEF. During an interview, he told me Viralheat was a must have for our organization. After looking through the website, I decided that Viralheat was exactly what I was looking for. I wanted a way that I could monitor what I was doing over the Web and across social media sites. I was using Facebook Insights, Tweetdeck, etc., but I didn't know what conversations were going on outside of Facebook and Twitter, and it was obvious that Viralheat would be a much more effective and efficient way for me to monitor our social sites. This way I could get more done in the day, instead of going through 1,000+ websites trying to track our presence! ("Viralheat offers . . . comprehensive tool to track Twitter, Facebook, Blogs, Websites, Pinterest and videos acros the social web, and tap into real-time social conversations." From Viralheat home page)

Social Media Challenges

I was brought in to DMEF as its first-ever social media intern. Although DMEF was registered under various social media sites, the staff was so busy that it was hard for them to keep up with all of it and that resulted in only small fan bases on these sites. The greatest challenge I faced was starting from the beginning, because we had such a small fan base, and it was my responsibility to both gain and engage followers. I couldn't just put up any article and have a significant number of people "like" it. I had to make sure that the content I was posting was interesting and relevant. It was very challenging to learn about who my audience was and what it took (the types of questions and content to post) for them to engage.

Results

Viralheat has been invaluable to the success of DMEF's social media engagement these past two months. Through Viralheat, I was able to track what type of content was popular and unpopular among my recent posts (love the sentiment tool), mostly through looking at the Twitter and real-time Web graphs and reports. I also found it very helpful in figuring out what content is popular in my industry. Along with creating a profile for my company, I created profiles for other nonprofits similar to ours that have a large social media presence. I used Viralheat to track what type of content was successful for them— then was able to mimic that on our social media sites. I am proud to say that since the start of my internship, our fan base on Twitter, Facebook and Linkedin has nearly doubled in size across all three communities.

Reprinted with permission: Viralheat.com

✳ ✳ ✳

Making Your Practice Perfect

Exercise: Select Your Tool(s)

Now comes the fun part—selecting the right tool or tools for you. Follow the steps below to complete your own evaluation of listening tools to pick the tool that best fits your needs.

Action 1: List Your Non-Negotiables

Write down elements or features that you absolutely must have. These are the things that are simply not negotiable based on your listening objectives and budget.

Action 2: Outline Your Comparison Chart

Outline your comparison chart to go through and compare or rate each major tool attribute. Again, these are:

1. Pricing structure
2. Media-type coverage
3. Access to historical data
4. Data portability
5. Usability
6. Integration with social accounts
7. Languages
8. Customer service
9. Special features

Our book website has a comparison template that you can download for this exercise (***http://TheSocialCurrent.com/resources***). The exact rating system will vary a bit from person to person, but the important thing is that you're determining which tool is best for your objectives. You might choose to rate each factor on a scale of 1 to 10, or you might just write down notes and pick a winner for each category. It's up to you, as long as the end result is that you have a clear case for why you are recommending one particular tool over the others in the end.

Action 3: Fill in Your Comparison Chart Notes for Each Tool That You Are Evaluating

We've put together a wiki to share findings across various listening tools, available at *http://TheSocialCurrent.com/wiki*. Use the notes from this wiki, along with your own demonstrations and research to fill in your comparison chart.

Action 4: Select the Tool or Tools That Best Align with Your Non-Negotiables

Now that you've completed your comparison chart, select the tool that best aligns with the non-negotiables and the other priorities that you've listed.

5

Setting Up Your Search Keywords

'How do I know,' the sometimes-despairing writer asks, 'which the right word is?' The reply must be: only you can know. The right word is, simply, the wanted one; the wanted word is the one most nearly true. True to what you ask? The answer is: Your vision and your purpose.

Elizabeth Bowen
Author
After-Thought: Pieces about Writing

In this chapter, you will learn:

- How to create a list of specific keywords to track your organization, competitors and special topics.

Essential Terms for Chapter 5

- **Boolean Search** (also called "Boolean Logic" or "Boolean Operators"): A set of keyword search rules that allows users to combine terms in order to search for relevant text.
- **Keywords:** A set of word combinations used to search for a particular topic or organization.

STEP 5—Setting Up Your Search Keywords

Setting up specific keywords to search for social media posts about your organization or industry in social media may very well be the most difficult part of your entire listening program. We've worked with brilliant industry veterans who struggle to come up with the right keywords to track brands, programs, competitors and industries. It's easy to come up with *concepts* to track, but it's much more difficult to come up with the specific keywords that will return relevant social media conversations surrounding those concepts. This part of the job will be hands-on, and you will need to evaluate your keywords on a regular basis to make sure they are up-to-date. It's a bit like a word game. Boggle, anyone?

First, you need to understand the basic structures of Boolean search logic—a set of rules that will help you conduct more refined and powerful searches. From there, we'll walk through the process for setting up your specific keyword list.

What Is Boolean Search?

For an explanation of Boolean logic and how it works, we turn to the following description provided by Jennifer Strickland and John R. Henderson, Ithaca College, New York:

> The principle of Boolean logic lets you organize concepts together in sets. When searching computer databases, including keyword searching of the online catalog, these sets are controlled by use of Boolean operators **OR**, **AND**, and **NOT**.
>
> But forget about libraries and computers for a moment and think about ice cream. Imagine all the possibilities a soft ice-cream machine could make if it offered just these three flavors—chocolate, strawberry, and vanilla—and could mix together any and all combinations of those flavors.
>
> There are seven possible combinations of ice cream flavors available: each flavor by itself (3), three combinations of two flavors in a swirl (3), plus all three flavors mixed together (1).
>
> **OR**
> In Boolean logic terms, a set that included any of these flavor combinations would be expressed:
>
> Strawberry OR vanilla OR chocolate

The Venn diagram for this combination would look like this:

In database searching, <u>OR</u> expands a search by broadening the set. It is often used to combine synonyms or like concepts. If you were interested in searching an online database for information about teenagers, to be more comprehensive you might use the set: **adolescents <u>OR</u> adolescence <u>OR</u> teens <u>OR</u> teenagers <u>OR</u> young adults**

This search statement would retrieve records that mention any of those terms. Think of <u>OR</u> as **either or**. The <u>OR</u> operator, however, doesn't have to group together synonyms. You could also search a database for "infants <u>OR</u> children <u>OR</u> adolescents."

AND

Thinking back on ice cream, if you don't wish to try every possible flavor combination the soft ice-cream machine can offer all at once, you must **narrow** your selection. You might want to choose an individual flavor or one combination of flavors. To order a swirl of all three flavors combined, chocolate, vanilla, and strawberry **all** must be included.

In terms of Boolean logic, a set that includes all three elements would be expressed as:

Strawberry AND vanilla AND chocolate

The Venn diagram for this combination would look like this:

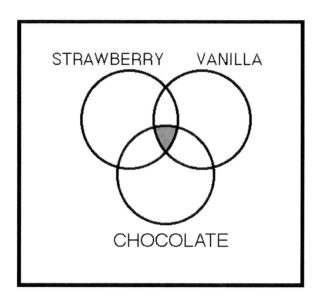

In database searching, **AND** narrows a search. It is often used for linking together different concepts. Searching a database with the search statement **college students AND behavior** would retrieve records only if both the phrase "college students" and the word "behavior" appear. Think of **AND** as **only if also**.

Please remember that the database is not doing any thinking, nor does it understand any concepts; it is only matching words and phrases. A record for an item that is principally about the economic status or religious beliefs of college students would be retrieved if the word "behavior" appears somewhere in the record, but an item about college students and drug use or alcohol abuse would not, unless the term "behavior" is included in the searchable part of the record.

NOT

Let's go back to the ice cream. You may hate chocolate. I know it may be hard to do, but pretend you hate chocolate. Perhaps you have already eaten three brownies and don't want any more chocolate. When you order ice cream, if you do NOT want chocolate, that would leave you with only three possibilities, strawberry by itself, vanilla by itself, or a swirl of strawberry and vanilla. In other words, you're subtracting a concept out of it. The resulting set would be:

(Strawberry OR vanilla) NOT chocolate

The Venn diagram for this combination would look like this:

In database searching, **NOT** is used to eliminate an unwanted concept. If you were interested in studying college students but not high school students, you could create a set **college students NOT high school.**

Keep in mind that **NOT** should be used sparingly, perhaps not at all, since it often brings about unintended results. Once again, remember that the database is not doing any thinking, nor does it understand any concepts; it only matches words. If you were interested in research on college students but not on research of high school students, you could add the concept <u>NOT</u> **high school** to your search statement. That would eliminate many records that are only about high school students, but it would also eliminate records that deal with both college students and high school students, such as this one: "**College students** are better prepared than students in boarding **high schools** to deal with the challenges of living away from home."

Combining Operators

You can combine sets in a variety of ways using the different combinations of Boolean operators. When writing out the sets, parentheses are important because they keep the logic straight. In the grouping (**high school students** <u>OR</u> **college students**) <u>AND</u> (**behavior** <u>OR</u> **motivation**) <u>AND</u> (**drugs** <u>OR</u> **alcohol**) the parenthesis around first set tells the database to create a final set of records that may include either of the phrases high school students OR college students, but only when the records also include either of the words "behavior OR motivation" plus only if in addition either of the words "drugs OR alcohol" appear.

Beyond Boolean (Truncation and Wild Cards)

In addition to using Boolean operators, for good searches, it may be necessary to use **truncation** and **wild card** characters to expand or control searches.

Truncation is a searchable shortened form of a word. This means you can take short cuts. Instead of writing out adolescents OR adolescence, you can use the truncated term adolescen*. Unfortunately, databases are not consistent with truncation symbols, so in one you might have to use adolescen*, but in another adolescen?, and in yet another, just adolescen (if truncation is automatic). Many databases are smart enough to pick up regular plurals without adding truncation, such as school retrieving both school and schools, but not all do, and they would be even less likely to be designed so that child would retrieve both child and children, without also retrieving childbirth, childhood, and childishness.

Wild card characters are useful because of alternate spellings and other quirks in the English language. Just as British and Canadian ice cream comes in **flavours**, not **flavors**, a British or Canadian study of college students may use the term **behaviour**, instead of **behavior**. Searching with a wild card can help. With the term **behavio?r**, both **behaviour** and **behavior** may be searched together. The most common use of wild cards is because of women. **Wom*n** should pick up both **women** and **woman**. Once again, because databases are not consistent with the characters they use, as the examples indicate, you will have to use different wild card characters in different databases. It is best to check the help screens to see the exact symbols and rules.

Reprinted by permission—Jennifer Strickland, Fine Arts Librarian and John R. Henderson, Social Sciences Librarian at Ithaca College (New York.)

Check your tool of choice for an advanced search guide to see which alternative symbols you should be using. For example, Twitter Search (http://twitter.com/search) has a full page of tips and operators below the search box, and Google offers a complete guide of search tricks and operators at *http://support. google.com/websearch*. If you can't find a search guide, look for an advanced search feature to help you structure the search.

Twitter Search Tricks

- from:twitteruser
  - ▸ Only return tweets from a specific user.
  - ▸ Example: "social media" from:mashable will return refer-

ences to the exact phrase "social media" from the user @mashable.

- filter:links
  - ▸ Only return Twitter posts with links.
  - ▸ Example: "case study" filter:links will return all tweets that reference the exact phrase "case study" that contain links. {{{See note below}}}

- to:username
  - ▸ Only return tweets sent to a particular Twitter user.
  - ▸ Example: "social media" to:mashable will return references to the exact phrase "social media" directed to @mashable. You can also search @username to search for replies, references and retweets (for example:"social media" @mashable).

- near:city
  - ▸ Only return tweets in a particular city.
  - ▸ Example: (event OR events) near:chicago will return references to events from Twitter users in the Chicago area.

- near:city within:30mi
  - ▸ Search within a certain range of a particular city.
  - ▸ Example: (event OR events) near:chicago within:30mi will return references to events from Twitter users within roughly 30 miles of the Chicago area. You can also substitute *mi* with *km* to search in kilometers.

- When using Twitter search, use "-" instead of NOT to remove words from your search. The "-" will also allow you to filter out from the searches above.
  - ▸ Example: "case study"—filter:links will return only tweets that mentioned the exact phrase "case study" without links.

Google Search Trick

- site:URL
  - ▸ Search for content within a specific website.
  - ▸ Example: "case study" site:mashable.com will return references to the exact phrase "case study" within the website mashable.com. This is a great trick for searching within blogs or websites that don't have their own inter-

nal search boxes. We use this trick when we're looking for bloggers to reach out to. It makes it easy to find out if they have previously referenced our organization, competitors or industry.

Pinterest Search Trick

- http://pinterest.com/source/url.com
    - ‣ Return all pins that have linked to a specific URL.
    - ‣ Example: http://pinterst.com/source/starbucks.com will return all pins that have linked to starbucks.com.

Setting up Search Terms to Find Conversations Around a Brand, Industry or Concept

When we're building out complex search queries around brands, industries or concepts, we like to use Twitter Search (http://twitter.com/search) to put keywords through a trial run and see if we're on the right track. Twitter Search will give you instant feedback on the context people actually use around your keywords, and it will usually lead you to discover new keywords. When setting up a keyword list, you'll want to consider the following overarching categories to return your initial results. Even if there are no results around your own brand at this point, you can use this exercise to better understand your competitors.

—**Organization Keywords:**
- Organization/brand name
- Casual references, misspellings and common Twitter hashtags
- Specific products
- Marketing tag lines and programs
- Twitter handle, website URL and other social properties (most search tools will return references to hashtags without the use of the "#" symbol)
- Leadership and spokespeople

—**Industry Keywords:**
- Competitors (go through the above categories for each competitor)
- Industry/category (optional)

Tracking Competitors and Industry Keywords

If you're planning to track specific competitors, go through the same exercise for each. You'll have to do some legwork to learn about each company's specific products, marketing programs and social/web properties. Company websites and Twitter Search will both be helpful here.

Inclusive and Exclusive Keywords

Next, think about whether each of your keywords can be represented with simple unique words that will return results that are relevant to your brand or organization (e.g., "mcdonald's"), or whether some words or phrases will compete with other concepts or companies that will return results that aren't relevant to you (e.g., mcd).

Again, use Twitter Search to determine whether most search results are relevant to what you are looking for, or whether the results return a high enough volume of irrelevant posts that they will need additional qualifiers to be refined further.

For example, if we search for the keyword "mcd" (which is the McDonald's symbol on the New York Stock Exchange), we may get results related to the Melbourne College of Divinity, a Seattle punk band called the Murder City Devils or references to the airport code for the Mackinac Island Airport in Michigan. To get more accurate results around this keyword, we need to make it inclusive by adding additional keywords to filter by or exclusive by filtering out keywords associated with irrelevant results.

Keyword Proximity

Some of the more sophisticated search tools allow users to search for keywords within a specific proximity to each other. For example, we may choose to search for "friendlie" AND "bank" within five keywords to find results that are not the exact phrase, but are close enough to produce relevant results (e.g., Friendlie National Bank). Otherwise, "friendlie" AND "bank"may return irrelevant results where the two words are paragraphs apart.

Avoid These Pitfalls When Building Your Keyword Lists

We commonly see two major pitfalls when we review keyword lists for companies.

1. Vague Keywords

Make sure you understand the difference between searching for general concepts and searching for actual references to those concepts in relation to your brand or industry. For example, we see a lot of lists that look like this:

- "mega burger"
- dinner
- lunch
- yum
- fries

See the problem? A search for a keyword like "dinner" will return all references to dinner, whether or not they involve your brand. Skip the vague keywords, and stick to words that will return results that matter to you. Hint: in most cases, if you follow the points presented for organization keywords and industry keywords listed above, you'll get results around these related concepts anyway).

2. Repetitive Keywords

When you're putting together a list of keywords to search, always try to keep it as simple as possible. For example, we see this all the time:

- "mega burger"
- "mega burger" AND dinner
- "mega burger" AND lunch
- "mega burger" AND yum
- "mega burger" AND fries

See the problem this time? If you are trying to monitor for references to Mega Burger, and you are already searching for variations on "mega burger," there is no need to include other searches that add on to this core phrase. Keep it as simple as possible for your overarching search. You can add these variations later when it comes time to set up more specific subcategories and alerts to monitor for.

Sample Keyword Lists

Let's walk through some potential keywords for each of our organizations. When you start building out your list, grab a blank piece of paper or blank document for brainstorming. Because keywords typically aren't case sensitive, we'll write everything out in lowercase to avoid confusion and distraction. It's important to note that your keyword list will serve as the starting point for searches, and that this list should be updated regularly.

Eco Redux Studio

1. **Core organization/brand name**
   "redux studio"
2. **Casual references, misspellings and common Twitter hashtags**
   ecoreduxstudio
   "redux studios"
   "redux studio's"
   "reduxe studio"
   "reduxe studios"
   "reduxe studio's"
   reduxestudio
   reduxestudios
   reduxestudio's
   reduxstudio
   reduxstudios
   reduxstudio's
3. **Specific products**
   "redux cotton"
   reduxcotton
   "redux jewelry"
   Reduxjewelry
4. **Marketing tag lines and programs**
   "redux responsibility"
   reduxresponsibility
   "reduxe responsibility"
   Reduxeresponibility
5. **Twitter handle, website URL and other social properties**
   reduxstudio.com
   Mary has reserved the Twitter handle @reduxstudio. Because reduxstudio is already in her keywords above, she already has this covered.
6. **Leadership and spokespeople**
   "mary osmand"
   maryosmand

7. **Competitors**

Go through the above categories for each competitor.

8. **Industry/category; examples include:**

"earth-friendly" AND apparel
"earthfriendly" AND apparel
"earth friendly" AND apparel
"earth-friendly" AND cloth
"earthfriendly" AND cloth
"earth friendly" AND cloth
"earth-friendly" AND clothes
"earthfriendly" AND clothes
"earth friendly" AND clothes
"earth-friendly" AND clothing
"earthfriendly" AND clothing
"earth friendly" AND clothing
"earth-friendly" AND fashion
"earthfriendly" AND fashion
"earth friendly" AND fashion
"eco-friendly" AND apparel
"ecofriendly" AND apparel
"eco friendly" AND apparel
"eco-friendly" AND cloth
"ecofriendly" AND cloth
"eco friendly" AND cloth
"eco-friendly" AND clothes
"ecofriendly" AND clothes
"eco friendly" AND clothes
"eco-friendly" AND clothing
"ecofriendly" AND clothing
"eco friendly" AND clothing
"recycled cotton"
"recycled water bottles" AND apparel
"recycled water bottles" AND cloth
"recycled water bottles" AND clothes
"recycled water bottles" AND clothing
"recycled water bottles" AND fashion
"sustainableapparel"
"sustainable apparel"
"sustainable cloth"
"sustainable clothes"
"sustainable fashion"

sustainableapparel
sustainablecloth
sustainableclothes
sustainablefashion
"sustainable apparel"
"sustainable cloth"
"sustainable clothing"
"sustainable fashion"

Similar keywords could be applied to concepts such as "product," "products" or other specific sustainable product categories.

Friendlie Bank

1. **Organization/brand name**
   friendlie AND bank (within five keywords)
2. **Casual references, misspellings and common Twitter hashtags**
   friendliebank
   friendly AND bank (within five keywords)
   friendly's AND bank (within five keywords)
   friendly'sbank
   friendlysbank
   friendlie's AND bank (within five keywords)
   friendliesbank
   friendlie'sbank
   friendlie AND banking (within five keywords)
   friendlie's AND banking (within five keywords)
   friendlies AND banking (within five keywords)
3. **Specific products**
   friendlie AND checking (within five keywords)
   friendly AND checking (within five keywords)
   friendlie's AND checking (within five keywords)
   friendlies AND checking (within five keywords)
   friendlie AND checks (within five keywords)
   friendly AND checks (within five keywords)
   friendlie's AND checks (within five keywords)
   friendlies AND checks (within five keywords)
   friendlie AND card (within five keywords)
   friendly AND card (within five keywords)
   friendlie's AND card (within five keywords)

friendlies AND card (within five keywords)

4. **Marketing tag lines and programs**
"a friendlie world"
afriendlieworld
friendlieworld
"a friendly world"
afriendlyworld
friendlyworld
"friendlie service"
friendlieservice

5. **Twitter handle, website URL and other social properties**
friendliebank.com
friendlieusa

6. **Leadership and spokespeople**
"eric friendlie"
ericfriendlie

7. **Competitors**
Go through the above categories for each competitor.

Mega Burger

1. **Organization/brand name**
"mega burger"

2. **Casual references, misspellings and common Twitter hashtags**
"mega burgers"
"mega burger's"
megaburger
megaburgers
megaburger's
"megga burger"
Meggaburger

3. **Specific products**
"megalicious burger"
megaliciousburger
"itty burger"
ittyburger
gigantaburger
giganta-burger

4. **Marketing tag lines and programs**
"mega taste"
megataste

5. **Twitter handle, website URL and other social properties**
megaburger.com

6. **Leadership and spokespeople**
"bob burgess"
bobburgess
"robert burgess"
robertburgess

7. **Competitors**
Go through the above categories for each competitor.

Hartlin Kids

1. **Organization/brand name**
"hartlin kids"

2. **Casual references, misspellings and common Twitter hashtags**
hartlinkids
hartlinkid
"heartlin kid"
"heartlin kids"
heartlinkids
"heartlin kid"
heartlinkid

3. **Specific products**
Hartlin Kids does not have any specific products.

4. **Marketing tag lines and programs**
"healthy habits. healthy kids"
healthyhabitshealthykids
"healthy habbits. healthy kids"
healthyhabbitshealthykids
"healthy habits healthy kids"
"healthy habbits healthy kids"
healthyhabbitshealhtykids

5. **Twitter handle, website URL and other social properties**
hartlinkids.com

6. **Leadership and spokespeople**
"sheila gordan"
sheilagordan
"shiela gordan"
shielagordan

7. **Competitors**
Go through the above categories for each competitor.

8. **Industry/category; examples include:**
child AND exercise
child AND obesity
child AND nutrition
childhood AND exercise
childhood AND obesity
childhood AND nutrition
children AND exercise
children AND obesity
children AND nutrition
school AND obesity
school AND nutrition
schools AND nutrition
schools AND obesity

Amy (Marketing Consultant)

1. **Organization/brand name**
"amy sanders"
2. **Casual references, misspellings and common Twitter hash-tags**
amysanders
3. **Specific products**
Amy does not have any specific products.
4. **Marketing tag lines and programs**
Amy does not currently have any tag lines or programs.
5. **Twitter handle, website URL and other social properties**
amysandersmarketing.com
6. **Leadership and spokespeople**
These keywords are already covered above.
7. **Competitors**
After she gets a chance to explore initial social conversations, Amy may choose to track specific industry leaders.
8. **Industry/category; examples include:**
"small business" AND marketing
"small businesses" AND marketing
"local business" AND marketing
"local businesses AND marketing
marketing AND conference
marketing AND conferences
marketing AND meetup near:chicago
marketing AND "meet up" near:chicago

marketing AND "meet-up" near:chicago
marketing AND event near: chicago
marketing AND events near: chicago
"social media" AND meetup near:chicago
"social media" AND "meet up" near:chicago
"social media" AND "meet-up" near:chicago
"social media" AND event near: chicago
"social media" AND events near: chicago (etc)

Next Steps: Set up Alert Keywords and Subcategories to Track Opportunities and Threats

Now that you have your basic keyword list set up, it's time to dive deeper and understand what consumers really care about. This will help us to create a list of keywords to track opportunities and threats in Chapter 9.

———————

CASE STUDY 5.1—How Perceptions Around Specific Words Help a Company Launch a New Line

The Challenge

Loudpixel was approached by a food company that was in the process of developing a new product line. The product line was still in the early stages of planning, and it had not yet been named or branded. After narrowing down a list of potential names and tag lines, the company asked the Loudpixel team to research perceptions around each specific word and concept that they were considering for the new product line. This information would be used to determine the best name for the new brand, along with associated tag lines.

The team was particularly interested in answering the following questions:

1. What concepts are these words most frequently associated with at this time?
2. Are there any risks associated with these words based on current context in social media conversations?

3. Are there any opportunities associated with these words based on current context in social media conversations?

The Approach

Loudpixel used each of the words and phrases that the brand was considering as keywords to pull relevant social media posts from the social media aggregation tool, Radian6. These social posts were imported into Levee, Loudpixel's analysis tool, as a representative sample set, and analysts evaluated the posts to determine the context and sentiment related to each of the words.

The Results

The team was able to understand trends and perceptions related to the words that the company was considering in association with the new brand. The company used this knowledge to select the words and phrases with the most positive associations to incorporate into the new brand naming and tag lines.

* * *

Making Your Practice Perfect

Exercise: Create Your Core Keyword List

Now it's your turn to create a search keyword list for your organization. If there aren't any conversations around your organization yet, just focus on your competitors. Use *http://twitter.com/ search* to test out your keywords and determine which words will need to be excluded from your searches to make the results more relevant. Go through each of the six keyword categories below for your organization and for your key competitors:

- Organization/brand name
- Casual references, misspellings and common Twitter hashtags
- Specific products
- Marketing tag lines and programs
- Twitter handle, website URL and other social properties

(most search tools will return references to hashtags without the use of the "#" symbol)
- Leadership and spokespeople

As you write your keywords out, be sure to write out your Boolean logic, including quotes around exact phrases, AND, OR, parentheses, truncation and wild card characters. Make the list so clear that anyone on your team could pick it up and duplicate your results exactly.

6

Social Media Analysis

Social analytics tools will become the must-have to gain insight, make better, faster business decisions and improve customer satisfaction.

—Social Business News

In this chapter, you will learn:

- How to use social media listening to answer specific questions about your business and to produce useful insights.
- How to select the listening methods you need to answer business questions and produce useful insights.
- How to identify spam and remove it and other irrelevant posts from your analysis.
- How to analyze social media conversations for context and sentiment.
- How to set program goals that can be tied to specific metrics for measurement.
- How to analyze reactions to your own social content to improve content creation.
- How to recognize the difference between strategic listening and tactical listening.

Essential Terms for Chapter 6

- **Affiliate Spam (also called "Blog Spam")**: Websites or blogs that are set up with the intention of linking to and selling products online. These sites automatically scrape text from other websites in order to pose as real blogs, but they typically contain no original content.

- **Benchmark Report:** An initial report that is used to understand an organization's current position and later to compare against future reports in order to determine progress.
- **Goal:** An objective that is specific, measurable and time-based, typically used to measure the outcomes of a particular program or strategy.
- **Key Performance Indicators (KPIs):** A specific set of metrics that can be tied to a goal, used to track the progress and, ultimately, measure the outcomes of a particular program or strategy.
- **Representative Sample Set:** Within the context of social media analysis, a representative sample set is a relevant set of social media posts that accurately reflects the trends of the total population as supported by appropriate statistical analysis.
- **Strategic Listening:** Monitoring and/or analyzing social media conversations in order to better understand customers and prospects, and to gain insights that influence the direction of business communication.
- **Tactical Listening:** Monitoring social media conversations in order to discover unique opportunities to promote the organization on a day-to-day basis.
- **Tag Cloud:** A visual representation of the most frequently used words within a data set; words that are used the most frequently are typically displayed proportionately larger than words that are used less frequently.
- **Tagging:** The act of adding words and sentiment to a set of social media posts in order to understand context and popular topics within the overall data set.

STEP 6—Getting Started with Social Media Analysis

At this point in the process, you have set your basic *listening objectives*, and you have selected a set of tools to help you meet these objectives. You've set up your overarching search keywords—the keywords you'll use to aggregate social posts about your brand, your competitors and your industry.

Now, you're ready to dive in and start making sense out of your social media data.

First, a word of caution: There is an old saying in business: good, fast, or cheap. You can have any two of these, but it's nearly impossible to have all three at once. This principle certainly applies to developing insights from social media data.

You can try to use automated analysis to get a quick, basic understanding of who your customers are and what they are saying, and you can use free or very inexpensive technology to help you do your job. But if you want high-quality results, there is no substitute for serious human analysis of the data you retrieve, and serious human analysis is neither fast nor cheap.

Let's take a look at a few examples.

The Pitfalls of Automated Analysis

Automated Analysis Pitfall 1:
Filtering Spam and Irrelevant Posts

Consider yourself lucky if your organization or brand has a unique name. For example, it will be much easier to return relevant search results around companies with names such as AirBnb, Boeing or Uniqulo than for companies like Apple, Uber or Gap—words that have additional meanings in common usage. Even companies with relatively unique names like Outback Steakhouse and Southwest Airlines require more complicated searches to capture casual references to the brands, such as "Outback" and "Southwest."

Since well begun is half done, it would be wise for a new business to select a unique name that is easy to search. This name should avoid the inclusion of common words or phrases that will send automated analysis off on a wild goose chase, pulling in off-topic social media posts and confounding your ability to easily track social media posts about the business.

In our experience, anywhere from 5% to 70% of search results for any given brand are a combination of off topic and spam posts, no matter how good the keywords are.

Retail brands are especially likely to attract affiliate spam posts. These are posts from Twitter users and blogs that are set up simply to drive traffic to e-commerce sites to make a profit. The accounts do not have any real engagement, but many search aggregators have a difficult time differentiating spam content from real people.

Brands that include common words or phrases, of course, are

more likely to have a higher percentage of irrelevant search results than unique names will have.

Tips for Identifying Spam Content

As you're reviewing social media posts in order to determine what is and isn't relevant to your organization, stay on the look-out for content created from affiliate spam accounts. These sites typically scrape content from other sites with the intention of driving traffic to an e-commerce site to make a portion of the final sale. If you see the warning signs below, you should eliminate the site from your content analysis.

- Check out the URL. If you see that the main URL is a string of mumbo-jumbo letters or numbers (for example, ab3bg.com/widgetreview), or if it's directly related to selling a particular product (for example, http://buywidgets. com/widgetreview) there's a good chance that you're looking at an affiliate website.
- Look for multiple posts with the same content. Retweets are one thing, but if you see a string of the same overly positive or promotional posts from different sites or Twitter users with no direct attribution, you're likely looking at affiliate spam.
- Look for specific keywords that are often associated with spam. Proceed with caution when you see words like "buy cheap," "buy now," "low price," "hot deals," "online shop," "Amazon" or other content that is overly promotional toward the brand or company. In fact, in many cases, you can filter these words out from the get-go, depending on the specific organization and your goals.
- Look for a string of positive reviews followed by links to Amazon. Affiliate sites will often repost positive reviews promoting a product, followed by a link to buy the product online.
- Look at the "About" page. Most affiliate blogs will be missing full content on their "About" pages. If you see the text "just another Wordpress blog," or words to that effect, on the "About" page, there's a fair chance that you're looking at spam.
- As a final check to see if a blog is spam, paste the blog URL into Compete.com or Quantcast.com to get a rough esti-

mate of the monthly unique visitors to the site. A traffic estimate won't tell you whether a blog is spam on its own—there are many blogs with low readership out there—but if the blog has other signs of being a spam site, and these traffic estimating services show that traffic is too low to estimate, you can be fairly certain that the blog is not relevant to your analysis.

- Use your best judgment. Sometimes affiliate spam is obvious, but sometimes it's not. The more you pay attention to the general design and features of these sites, the better able you'll be to identify them.

Automated Analysis Pitfall 2: Automated Sentiment Analysis Is Only as Good as the Humans Reviewing It.

Automated sentiment, or "natural language" analysis as it is sometimes called, is becoming more sophisticated every day, but as we mentioned in Chapter 4, it is far from a flawless science. Natural language processing is the underlying technology that allows computers to derive, interpret and report on the meaning behind the human language it processes.

British research firm FreshMinds pitted automated analysis versus human analysis of social media sentiment in a study it conducted to determine the accuracy of both free and paid social media search tools. They found that automated sentiment analysis is essentially worthless without human involvement. In fact, automated sentiment analysis alone showed to be no more accurate in identifying true sentiment from social media feeds than simply flipping a coin.

The power and wide-reaching abilities of social media search tools (both free and paid) make them an essential part of any social media monitoring plan, but for all their bells and whistles, these automated search tools cannot completely replace the abilities of a human.

> While humans don't come close to competing with machines in terms of search capacity and processing mass amounts of data in a short period of time, there are aspects of monitoring where machines cannot completely replace the quality of a smart, well trained, and careful human analyst,

and those aspects also happen to be the most important.

For more information, google this phrase: "FreshMinds automated versus human analysis."

Technology will only take you so far. Enter at your own risk.

Automated Analysis Pitfall 3: Automation Misses Nuance, Sarcasm and Irony.

This point is related to the previous one about the flawed nature of automated sentiment analysis. It deals with a particular way that certain subtleties of the language, what we might call nuanced language, tricks the automated system into thinking good is bad and vice versa.

These tools often analyze the sentiment or meaning of a word or group of words based on a set of "positive" or "negative" keywords. Posts that cannot be associated with these particular emotion- or expression-based keywords are either marked as neutral or unknown. Based upon our experience, neutral or unknown posts tend to be the majority of posts that these tools identify.

In Chapter 4, we provided examples of improperly categorized social posts related to Netflix, the online TV and movie-streaming service. Here are a few more examples of posts, this time related to Starbucks Coffee, that automated sentiment analysis has identified as negative. See if you can pick out the words or phrases that have triggered these inaccurate categorizations.

—I'm so sad that there isn't a Starbucks close by :(
—The worst part of my day is when my Starbucks drink is empty.
—I want Starbucks :(
—I love my roommate. She brought me Starbucks because I'm sick.
—I really wish we had a Starbucks here.
—I am hardly a coffee drinker, but that Starbucks just gave me my second wind! Definitely needed that!
—I'm in a really bad mood today. The only thing that will make me feel better is Starbucks.
—Wow. A customer at the Starbucks drive-thru paid for the five cars behind her, and I was a recipient of her generosity!

Words and symbols such as "sad," "worst," "sick," "bad" and frowning emoticons may automatically trigger negative sentiment, but a human can detect these inaccuracies right away.

Sarcasm is an area of language where automated analysis struggles. We define sarcasm as a sharp or bitter remark that is normally conveyed through irony. The irony in the remark is what makes sarcasm particularly hard to detect. Irony normally involves pretending ignorance that allows you to say one thing and mean something different. Hence, the difficulty an automated system has in detecting it.

Starbucks tag cloud

Take a look at the following examples. This time, automated sentiment analysis marked the posts as positive:

—Thank you Starbucks for my wonderfully burnt tongue this morning.
—Burnt coffee is soooooo good! Shout out to the lady at Starbucks who burned my coffee.
—OMG! You have a giant Starbucks coffee. You must really enjoy burnt milk.

This time, words such as "wonderfully," "good" and "enjoy" have led the machine to wrongly categorize these posts as positive.

Automated Analysis Pitfall 4: Discovering Context and Trends in Social Conversations.

Most automated analysis tools offer tag clouds or other keyword groupings to show the keywords that are used the most frequently in relation to an organization or concept.

The trouble is that if we look only at frequently used keywords, we often miss the ability to evaluate the underlying concepts and trends associated with these keywords. Tag clouds and keyword analysis can be helpful if time is of the essence, but if your listening objective is to answer a specific set of questions about how your customers feel about your brand, competitors or industry in order to uncover opportunities and threats, keyword analysis may not cut it. Let's take a look at a sample tag cloud based on Starbucks.

Starbucks Sample Tag Cloud

In the tag cloud, we see words like "favorite," "worse," "good" and "better." But just what do these words really mean to us? Beyond the lack of deeper context, different words with the same meaning may not be grouped together if they are spelled slightly differently. Take the following tweets, for example:

—I love the Starbucks app for iPhone. Digital Starbucks card and auto reload!

—I carry my Starbucks cards with me everywhere I go.

—I'm officially a Starbucks gold member!

—@Starbucks why does an electronic free reward need to expire? That's annoying.

—If you get Starbucks rewards, you'd better use them or lose them. You now have only about 5 weeks to use or they take them back. #StarbucksFail

All five posts are referring to Starbucks rewards, but each post uses a slightly different word to describe the concept: card, cards, gold, reward and rewards.

Because tag clouds are based on keyword frequency rather than concepts, even the largest word in a cloud may only make up a small percentage of overall posts, leading to a sense that any given topic may be more or less important than it actually is. For example, in the cloud above, no single word makes up more than 3% of total posts about Starbucks.

Finally, tag clouds typically do not take article sources into account, so a post from a Twitter user with one follower will be weighted the same as a post from a mainstream outlet with millions of readers.

The Pitfalls of Human Analysis

If the machine is imperfect, surely the solution is to have a human do all of the analysis instead, right?

Not so fast.

Some organizations (and concepts) have thousands or hundreds of thousands of social media posts and articles being shared about them each day—far more than any human, or even team of humans, could reasonably be expected to analyze. Why? Let's take a look at a few of the specific disadvantages of human analysis.

Human Analysis Pitfall 1: The Cost—It's More Expensive.

Adding a human layer to any analysis will always cost more, of course. Humans simply can't handle the scale that a computer can, and human analysis of social media posts requires competent, trained staff to read through posts and articles to remove irrelevant and spam posts, to make sense of the data and to report findings back to the team.

Human Analysis Pitfall 2: Time—It Takes Longer.

Automated analysis is nearly instantaneous. After your keywords are entered, you're just a click away from a keyword tag cloud or a pie chart showing estimated sentiment breakdown (though, as we know, the value of this automated analysis by itself is questionable, at best).

Human analysis, on the other hand, takes time. It requires an individual or team to read through posts and articles, tag them for context and identify trends. This process, by itself, would rarely be fast or complete enough to identify an impending crisis, for example, in time to prevent it.

Human Analysis Pitfall 3: Reliability—People Don't Always Mark Sentiment the Same.

In any content analysis process where more than one human analyst (or "coder") is involved in identifying and sorting data, intercoder reliability (the degree to which there is agreement among those doing the sorting and coding) is a key issue. Human sentiment analysis is a form of content analysis, which is, by definition, subjective activity.

A recent Mashable.com post reviewed a study on a set of

posts analyzed by people through Amazon's crowd-sourcing marketplace, Mechanical Turk. The study revealed that human analysts only agreed on sentiment 79% of the time. Trained coders on a content analysis research project are generally thought to be capable of proceeding with their analysis once they reach 90% inter-coder reliability. (For study details, see http://mashable.com/2010/04/19/sentiment-analysis.)

In another test of human coding reliability, this one run by Visible®, experienced professionals who tagged a set of social posts agreed with each other on sentiment 74% of the time. (For study details, see http://www.visibletechnologies.com/resources/case-studies/testing-sentiment-accuracy.)

Based on these findings, it's clear that even with human analysis, a team should not jump into tagging posts for sentiment without some pre-planning to determine how to handle particular topics.

Finding the Balance Between the Human and the Machine

There is no single, simple answer to the question of what is the "correct" blend of automated versus human analysis of social media. Ultimately, it will be up to each business team to establish listening objectives, determine which questions need to be answered, identify available financial and human resources, and figure out the right balance.

One thing is obvious. Neither automated nor human analysis of social media sentiment is perfect (or anywhere near perfect, for that matter). But, before you become disappointed by the pitfalls of both methods and throw up your hands in frustration, we want to share some good news with you.

If you want to get a more accurate understanding of the context and sentiment of social media conversations, but there are too many posts and articles for your team to reasonably analyze, we have a solution for you.

First, think about the last time you heard about a national study in the news:

—20% of small businesses in the U.S. allocate increasing budget for digital marketing.
—55% of people prefer to read email on a tablet.
—72% of 24 to 32 year-olds own smart phones.

All of these studies discuss a percentage of a greater population. Do you really think that these researchers surveyed every last individual within these populations? No way. They surveyed representative samples—a number of individuals sufficient to statistically represent the overall population. This sampling method provides researchers an efficient way to get an accurate view of a target population's opinion. Researchers use this same method to establish unemployment rates, collect television ratings and conduct political polling. In each case, a statistical sample represents the opinion or sentiment of a larger population.

If you have more posts to analyze than a team of humans can reasonably evaluate, you're in luck. You can use a representative sample set to get a deeper level of accuracy and context from these conversations without hiring an entire army of researchers to get the job done.

Creating a Representative Sample Set of Social Media Posts

In Chapter 4, we talked about data portability. If you're working with a social media aggregator that allows you to export your data to CSV (comma-separated value), you'll be able to create your own sample set with that data.

You say you don't have the confidence in your math skills to proceed? Don't fret. Go to *http://surveysystem.com/sscalc.htm* and enter the total number of posts you have collected in your "population" (the total number of social posts being returned in your search). The system will determine how many posts you will need to evaluate in your sample set in order to be reasonably confident that your findings represent what you'd find if you evaluated all the posts in the set.

You will need to understand two basic concepts about your sample set:

—**Confidence Level:** The confidence level will tell you how close the analysis of your sample is to what you would expect to find if you analyzed every post in your entire population. We typically seek a sample size large enough to give us a confidence level of 95%, which means that we are 95% certain that the analysis of the sample we have selected represents the total population.

—**Confidence Interval:** The confidence interval, or margin of error, will tell you the possible sampling error of your results. We typically use a confidence interval of 5, so if we find that 50% of social posts are being driven by a specific brand initiative, we are 95% confident that between 45% (50 minus 5) and 55% (50 plus 5) of all social posts from the entire population are being driven by that brand initiative.

Creating a Random Sample Set

Excel can be set up to select a random set of posts to analyze based on your sample size, but if you don't have the ability to set this up for yourself, another option is to divide your total population by the number of posts that will need to be analyzed, and tag the posts at that interval. For example, if you have 4,000 total posts to analyze with a sample size of 351, tag every 11th post in your set.

Don't worry if the math doesn't work out to a whole number when you divide it. Simply round it down. It's OK if you tag a few more posts than the sample recommends, as long as you tag the minimum number in the sample.

Getting Started with Content Analysis

Before you begin your in-depth research to understand the context and trends behind social media posts related to your organization, competitors or industry, look back at your listening objectives from Chapter 3, and determine the following:

—What specific questions are we trying to answer through social listening?
—What time frame will we analyze?

Carefully go through the list of questions that you want to answer. It's OK to keep a side list of some other observations you might be making along the way (things, for example, that you'd like to study later), but it's much more important at this phase to (as we have said before) to *keep the main thing the main thing*!

These questions, which are based upon your specific objectives, will be used to drive how you tag specific articles within your social media data stream or sample set for context. For example, if one of your objectives is to understand how people talk about specific customer service issues, you will tag your data set for specific areas of customer service.

If your industry is seasonal, you may want to start by analyzing a full year to understand how the context of the conversation changes throughout the year. Later, we'll discuss setting up a regular reporting schedule to compare changes across time.

Here's an important point made by social media researcher, Rebecca Denison:

> The biggest mistake any company can make when first starting social media listening is to look for what they already know. If you approach social media listening by looking for conversations about your brand or company that you expect, you may miss out on a whole different conversation, one you could learn from. It's important to go into social media listening assuming you don't know what you don't know. Sometimes it's hard to accept that everyone doesn't think of your brand or talk about your brand the way you want, but you have to be willing to accept that in order to fully understand how people perceive and discuss your brand in social media.

Tagging Social Articles for Context

Let's say that you have used your chosen social media aggregator to pull a set of social media posts related to your topic of interest. You've created a sample set of articles to evaluate within Excel or another tool of choice. Now what?

It's time to categorize your social articles for meaning, a process called "tagging." Tagging articles for context and sentiment requires some planning. This step will allow you to categorize your social posts and articles in a much more customized, specific way than if you just went at it haphazardly.

When we first started to analyze social media for context, we had the crazy idea that we could simply read through all of the posts and assign each one a single word to represent the context of the entire article. We quickly learned that this was a huge mistake. No single tag would allow us to evaluate trends and overlays in our data, and no one word could cover the meaning behind an entire article.

For example, rather than looking only at keywords, such as "worse" and "better" in the Starbucks tag cloud described previously, we may choose to create tags to break out any of the following categories and subcategories:

—Brand initiatives versus organic conversations:
  • Posts driven by specific advertising campaigns
  • Posts driven by specific spokespeople
  • Posts driven by specific sponsorships or events
  • Posts that contain key messages
  • Posts that contain specific tag lines
—Product attributes:
  • Posts driven by specific products or flavors
  • Posts driven by specific product attributes
—Organization visibility:
  • Posts where the organization is the main feature
  • Posts where the organization is mentioned as an aside (insignificant to the greater post or article)
  • Posts where the organization is mentioned in association with competitors
  • Posts driven by key media outlets or popular users (as defined by your organization)
—Customer service:
  • Specific customer service issues
—Consumer feelings and intent:
  • Posts that contain reviews
  • Posts that contain intent to buy
  • Posts that contain recommendations
—Social sharing:
  • Posts that contain links
  • Posts that contain hashtags
  • Posts that contain replies
  • Posts driven by retweets
—Demographics:
  • Location (city, state, region, country)
  • Male versus female
  • Media outlets (news outlet, pop culture outlet, trade outlet, etc.)
  • General age (you might identify this as an estimated age range, such as 15-24, 25-34, 35-44, 45-54 or 55+; these

ranges may vary based on your specific organization and goals)
- Ethnicity
- Other identifiable characteristics (e.g., student, parent, urban, rural, brand/category enthusiast, etc.)

Any of these categories could have a number of subcategories. Let's take a look at a few examples.

Eco Redux Studio

> I love the new fall collection from Eco Redux Studio. I can't wait to get my hands on those redux cotton yoga pants #sustainability

Any of the following tags could be applied to add context to this post:

—Fall collection
—Specific product
—Redux cotton
—Yoga pants
—Intent to buy
—Sustainability
—Hashtag
—Brand affinity
—Feature

This social media user is specifically discussing "intent to buy" the "Redux cotton" "yoga pants," a "specific product" from the "fall collection. The post includes a "hashtag" that specifically mentions "sustainability." The "feature" tag shows that the post features Eco Redux Studio, rather than comparing it to other brands or discussing the organization as an aside. Finally, this social user is sharing her "brand affinity" by proclaiming her love for the brand's products.

Friendlie Bank

> Thanks to the Friendlie Bank team for taking care of my stolen credit card so quickly #friendlieservice.

Any of the following tags could be applied to add context to this post:

—Customer service
—Stolen card
—Brand initiative
—Tag line
—Friendlie service
—Hashtag
—Feature

If you consider closely, these terms have several possible relationships. "Stolen card" could be a subcategory of "customer service," and both "tag line" and "Friendlie service" could be specific subcategories of "brand initiative." Similarly, "feature" could be used to show that the post features Friendlie Bank, rather than comparing it to other brands or discussing the organization as an aside.

Mega Burger

> Mega Burger's Gigantaburger is the most delicious thing I've ever tasted. Highly recommended. Much better than the tiny burgers at Sander Burgers.

Any of the following tags could be applied to add context to this post:

—Product attribute
—Gigantaburger
—Review
—Taste
—Recommendation
—Sander Burgers
—Burger size
—Comparison

In this case, "product attribute" signifies that the article is driven by a reaction to a product, in this case the "Gigantaburger." The post offers a casual "review" of the product, including a reference to "taste" and a "recommendation" to others. The message mentions competitor "Sander Burgers," specifically referencing the small "burger size." This is a "comparison" where the two brands are mentioned together rather than a "feature" of Mega Burger as the only brand in the entire post.

Hartlin Kids

> Junk Food Laws May Help Curb Childhood Obesity: Read more about the study at http://www.huffingtonpost.com/2012/08/13/study-junk-food-laws-may-_n_1771352.html

Any of the following tags could be applied to add context to this post:

—Laws
—Childhood obesity
—Research
—Linked article
—The Huffington Post
—Harvard Medical School

We prefer to tag posts that link to full articles as "linked article" along with the source of the article (in this case, the article is from "The Huffington Post"). This way, we can see which media outlets and blogs are driving the most conversations throughout the social web. Because this post also references "research" about "childhood obesity," we like to follow the link to find out the source of the research being mentioned (in this case, the source is "Harvard Medical School").

After tagging a full set of social posts related to the topics of children and exercise, obesity and nutrition, the Hartlin Kids team will be able to determine which news outlets and which research studies are driving the most buzz in social media. This information will help them to fulfill one of Hartlin Kids's main goals from Chapter 3: "We will determine which specific outlets or individuals are driving conversations in social media around topics related to childhood health, nutrition and exercise in order to start building relationships with them."

Amy: Marketing Consultant

> Infographic: 7 Keys to Being a Small Business Influencer. (http://bit.ly/7keysinfluence http://fb.me /1OCQsSlfK)

Any of the following tags could be applied to add context to this post:

—Infographic
—Image
—Linked article
—Laurarubinstein.com
—Influencer marketing
—Expert advice
—Numbered list

We like to track posts that contain images or link to images, which is why we've noted both the "infographic" and "image" that the post links to. This will help Amy to determine the elements that tend to get shared the most across the social web in relation to small business marketing. For example, is content more likely to be shared if it contains an image? Like the Hartlin Kids example, this post contains a "linked article" from "Laurarubinstein.com." This article is "expert advice" that specifically covers "influencer marketing" and is presented in a "numbered list."

Also like Hartlin Kids, Amy could tag a full sample set of posts to determine which media outlets or blogs are referenced the most often in relation to small business marketing and use this to fulfill one of her core goals: "I will track popular blogs related to small business marketing in order to start engaging and building relationships for future guest posts."

By tagging for topic categories rather than key words, you'll be able to correlate much larger conversation trends than can be seen through key word trends alone. For example, social posts related to your organization's own brand initiatives and messaging might account for 50% of all organization mentions, but because references to specific brand messages use different keywords, a tag cloud would not be able to capture this information.

Tagging Social Articles for Sentiment

Before your team begins tagging, sit down and go through the data to get a basic feel for the types of posts coming through in the search results. Determine as a team how to tag for sentiment. Here are a few factors to consider.

Sentiment Based on Reader Influence

One approach to tagging sentiment is to tag based on how each post may make the reader *feel about the organization or brand*. This approach will be more useful if one of your objectives is to measure how a specific initiative has influenced perceptions related to your organization that might result in a decision to purchase your product.

- Positive: The reader is more likely to purchase after reading the post.
- Neutral: The reader is neither more nor less likely to purchase after reading the post.
- Negative: The reader is less likely to purchase after reading the post.

Sentiment Based on Writer Feelings

Another approach is to tag based on how the *writer feels about the organization or brand*. This approach will be more useful if one of your objectives is to simply understand how consumers feel about your organization.

- Positive: The writer show positive feelings toward the organization.
- Neutral: The writer does not show positive or negative feelings toward the organization.
- Mixed: The writer shows both positive and negative feelings toward the organization.
- Negative: The writer shows negative feelings toward the organization.

Let's take a look at a few examples where sentiment tagging could vary, depending on your objectives:

> I'm at Starbucks.

The post above may be marked as neutral if you are tagging from a reader influence perspective; the reader is not necessarily more likely to purchase Starbucks after reading this post, since the post does not contain any specific facts about the organization that may make it any more or less desirable.

If your team is tagging based strictly on the expressed or presumed feelings of the writer, however, the post may be tagged as positive, since the writer is showing an affinity for the company by patronizing the store.

Let's look at another example:

> I want Starbucks.

Again, the post above may be marked as neutral from a reader influence perspective, since it does not contain any messages that may influence the reader to want Starbucks as well, besides basic brand awareness.

But again, from the writer's perspective, the post is clearly positive.

You can see why both automated sentiment analysis *and* human analysis will be inconsistent without planning up front. There are decisions that have to be made and well stuck to if your analysis is going to be successful. Fail to plan, and you plan to fail.

Tagging Sentiment by Topic

In cases where sentiment is mixed, you may choose to tag each topic with its own sentiment. For example, if two separate organizations are being compared, are both referenced with positive sentiment? Is one statement positive and one negative? You may consider adding a sentiment tag for each organization if your objective is to understand how your organization is perceived compared to your competitor.

Tagging Sentiment for Coupon Posts

Another sentiment topic that causes confusion among teams is coupon posts. If you work with a brand that may be tied to online coupons, sit down to discuss how your team will handle tagging sentiment for posts about coupons before you begin your analysis. For example, some teams will see the distribution of coupons as a positive. The reader is more likely to purchase a product or service after having seen a coupon. However, other teams may view coupons as neutral because the writer is simply sharing a deal and is not necessarily sharing specific positive feelings toward the organization. It is up to the team to decide how to handle this topic, but make sure tagging is consistent.

Diving Back into the Data

After your data is tagged for context, you will be ready to begin what is called a *discovery* or *benchmark* report to understand trends in social conversations around your company, competition and/or industry. During your first report, we recommend that you start by looking at general trends related to your organization or industry and then make a list of more specific questions that come out of these initial findings. From there, you may have to dive into a more specific set of keywords to answer all of your questions in full.

Go to *http://TheSocialCurrent.com/resources* to download a sample spreadsheet of tagged posts and see how we have calculated the trends to be used for the benchmark report.

Quantitative versus Qualitative Research Findings

As discussed in Chapter 2, researchers generally use two different styles of market research: quantitative and qualitative research. The type of research they choose to use is governed by a variety of factors and forces. Quantitative research (as in quantity) produces findings that are measured in numbers. Qualitative research (as in quality) is most often represented by words that are used to describe feelings and context.

Evaluative versus Formative Research

Market researchers have a number of reasons for doing research. We most often think of research within the context of evaluation. We use it to determine whether a program we have put in place is working or not. We use it to judge performance and to pay commissions and to make decisions about retaining or promoting employees.

Formative research, on the other hand, is used to help us develop campaigns. We use formative research to see what messages resonate, and often to listen to our customers to tell us what they like about our products so we can advertise these qualities, and what they don't like about our products so we can fix them. (For more discussion on these topics, go to Chapter 2.)

Correlation Versus Causation

As you start to look through your contextualized data for trends and correlations in data, always ask yourself "Why?" and "So what?" Be very careful that you understand how often people confuse correlation with causation. Children do this all the time. They assume that because two things seem to happen around the same time, one thing must have caused the other. We know better, but we oftentimes make childlike assumptions about the things we experience at or near the same time because we forget the difference between correlation and causation.

- Correlation: Two things occur at or around the same time and/or place.
- Causation: One cause produces one or more effects.

Here's a classic example: A person notices that when the sky is dark, more people have umbrellas with them. Does this mean that carrying umbrellas causes the sky to become dark? No. The cause of people carrying their umbrellas, in this case, is actually a third factor—the likelihood of rain. People understand that the umbrellas don't cause the rain. They probably also understand that the dark skies don't cause the rain either. But they do understand that dark skies are a signal that the rain may be coming, and this knowledge causes them to find their umbrellas and carry them.

Here's another common example: Social media mentions related to our organization have increased by 100% over the past year during a time at which our social media budget increased by 50%. Does this mean that every percent increase in our social media marketing budget caused an increase of two percent of social media mentions related to our organization? The answer is maybe yes or maybe no. It's highly likely that outside factors contributed as well.

In general, we know that social media usage is rising each and every year, regardless of what any individual organization is doing. So, what we may be seeing in the increase in mentions is not necessarily due to any specific action we are taking or took, but rather it may be due to the natural increase in users of all social media platforms, which would trigger a natural increase in mentions. Or, it may be due to the degree to which those people using social media each year are getting more fully engaged in it and more active in it, therefore "mentioning" more.

To identify causation—in other words, to be able to say for sure that our 50% increase in social media funding resulted in a 100% increase in social media mentions (or some portion of the increase)—our team would need to look at a large number of factors. For example, what is the context behind conversations that have been occurring behind social media, and to what degree might they be directly referencing the brand initiatives that are expressed through our increased budget?

Even in the best-case scenario, there will always be gray areas when we are attempting to "determine causality," as the social scientists might say.

For example, let's say that your organization hires a popular professional athlete to become an official spokesperson for the brand. On every game day, positive social media mentions related to the brand increase. These references will likely include direct mentions of the popular athlete in relation to the brand and indirect references to the brand that don't mention the athlete. You might be able to identify a direct cause and effect relationship between mentions of the athlete and the number of positive brand mentions on game day, but since so many factors are involved, you may have a difficult time pinpointing just exactly how many of the positive brand mentions are directly caused by the athlete's endorsement. And, therefore, it would be difficult to put an exact dollar value on just how many of the additional brand mentions can be attributed to the popular athlete, or how much would be a fair payment to make to him for the increased brand engagement.

These things are never perfect, and they are rarely easy. But we, at least, can demonstrate some positive relationship between the brand and the athlete, and vice versa, and that's a good thing for everyone.

Tying Social Analysis to Other Research and Data Points

Each type of research has its own bias built into it.

Surveys may suffer from selection bias—how we picked our sample—or question bias.

Focus groups may suffer from selection bias, moderator bias or the bias caused by a member of the group with strong opinions who dominates the discussion.

Social media research will suffer from selection bias that is based on who is using social media at any current period in history or at the specific time of day at which we are looking at the data.

For example, if you are hearing more 18 to 24 year olds talking positively about your organization in social media than 55 to 64 year olds, does that mean that one age group cares more about your brand than the other? Not necessarily. It would more likely mean that you have been listening to more young people than older ones because more of the younger ones are using the social media networks that you are listening to. You need to think about this in a different way.

A better way to evaluate this breakdown may be to look at the overall percentage of positive versus negative mentions within each age group. For example, there may be four thousand 18 to 24 year olds who are talking positively about your organization while another six thousand are talking it down (50% more negative posts than positive). At the same time, there could be two thousand 55 to 64 year olds who are talking positively about your brand while only 100 are talking negatively about it (1,900% more positive posts than negative).

This information could affect everything from how you are making and marketing your product to how you are servicing it after the sale. As a whole, you simply have to allow your data points to work together to round out your total understanding of your customers, and you have to work at removing the biases from each point of research.

In some cases, one form of research may drive another. For example, you may use social media research to drive the specific questions that you will ask in a survey or focus group. And as we said before, you'll be using all forms of research both to redesign your products and the messages you use to sell them—formative research—and to measure the impact of your messages and other strategies—the evaluative research.

SWOT Analysis

After gathering findings from social media and other research, put together a SWOT analysis to present your organization's Strengths, Weaknesses, Opportunities and Threats based on your social media listening findings.

Create a simple chart with four separate quadrants, and outline findings for each category. These findings will be used to help you develop and drive your strategic recommendations for the organization.

Strengths	Weaknesses
Opportunities	Threats

Program Measurement

Measurement reporting—what we have identified as the evaluative research—will be presented in a slightly different format from basic discovery, or formative research reports, though the approach to collecting the data is often very similar.

Evaluation is an ongoing process. Your team needs to decide how often to measure and to report findings in a way that helps to illustrate the impact of your programs and that allows you sufficient time to make adjustments to make your social media activity more effective.

Benchmarking and Ongoing Reporting

When it comes to measurement, we often get questions like these:

—Which is better, a Facebook comment or a blog comment?
—How much is a Twitter follower worth?
—I have 10,000 Facebook fans. Is this good?

Measurement requires context. You must have points of comparison in order to know whether or not you're making any progress. For example, let's say that you decided that you're going to get into better physical shape. You go out and run a mile in nine minutes. Is this a good time? Without context, it's hard to say. To get a better understanding of whether you're doing well, you need to compare yourself against at least one of two points:

1. Yourself over time
2. Yourself against a competitor

Your nine-minute mile may become a part of your fitness benchmark. Let's say you run a mile a day, every day of each week, and log your average mile time each Sunday. As your Sunday times improve, you have points on a chart against which to compare your progress.

As another option, you may join a running club and find a few running buddies who are similar in conditioning and age to you. You get together each Sunday and run a mile race. By comparing your Sunday times against the times of your running buddies, you will have a different context to understand whether your own running time is "good."

Brands work the same way. In order to measure progress, you need a baseline point of comparison—either a comparison against yourself over time or a comparison against direct competitors.

By the way, the issue of just who is a direct competitor is essential. Remember what we said earlier. It's extremely difficult, if not impossible, to have the fastest or most innovative, cheapest and the highest quality product or campaign in the marketplace.

Each company must decide what its essential discipline is and then strive to be the best at that. If your customers are patronizing your website because the company is known to have the absolute best after-sales service and return policy, chances are they are not looking for the absolute cheapest-priced product. If you try to be all things to all people, you'll probably end up being nothing to everybody.

Setting S.M.A.R.T. Goals

You've heard it said before, and if you haven't, you should have by now: If you don't know where you are going, any road will take you there.

In order to measure your progress in social media, or any other aspect of your business over time, you simply have to set specific goals for yourself.

Each goal you set should follow the *S.M.A.R.T.* model:

- Specific
- Measurable
- Attainable
- Realistic
- Time Based

Every goal you set for your organization needs to align with each of these areas. For example, "Increase positive social media mentions related to the brand by 50% from quarter one to quarter two" is a measurable goal.

"Getting more people to like our brand" isn't.

Tying Goals to Specific Metrics

Once you have determined your specific, measurable goals, it's time to determine which metrics you will use to measure the goals over time. These metrics, or key performance indicators (KPIs), should tie directly to each goal. For example:

- Goal 1: Increase positive social media mentions related to the brand by 50% from quarter one to quarter two.
  Metric: Number of positive mentions related to the brand during the first quarter of the year compared to the second quarter of the year over this 90+ day period.

- Goal 2: Increase online sales from social media by 5% from quarter one to quarter two.
  Metric: Number of dollars in sales leads driven by social media during the first quarter of the year compared to the second quarter of the year (note that only about 5% of all retail sales take place online, so most organizations will not be able to tie web analytics and click-throughs directly to sales numbers).

Begin by Analyzing and Optimizing Your Own Content

Beyond analyzing general reactions to your organization, competitors and industry in social media, you can also use social media analysis to understand how your customers and prospects are reacting to your social media content in order to make changes and improvements.

Here are some examples.

Facebook

By tracking fan reactions to your content on Facebook, you'll be able to better deliver content that resonates with this audience. You should be tracking both quantitative actions, such as likes and shares, as well as qualitative context, such as the context of comments on your posts and wall.

By using Facebook Insights or a Facebook-specific data platform such as PageLever.com, you can get to know your audience better in order to deliver more relevant content.

For example, what is the demographic makeup of your existing fans? In other words, what is the breakdown of gender, age groupings, ethnicity, income levels, etc.? And how do these various categories cross reference with one another? For example, do you have more men than women visiting your site, but the average age of the women is 27 and the average age of the men is 54?

We worked with one brand that saw a spike in lost Facebook fans during Breast Cancer Awareness Month. It turned out that the majority of their fans were young men, and messages related to breast cancer didn't resonate with this section of their audience. Make sure your messaging aligns with your fan base. Lost fans can be just as revealing about the impact of your strategy as new fans are.

You can also use free tools like EdgeKick.com to gauge how your organization compares to others in your business sector on Facebook. Create a spreadsheet to track average and median likes, people talking and new likes per day compared to average and median posts per week and types of posts from each organization (photos, videos, links, etc.). This will help you to get a better understanding of what is possible within your sector, as well as what types of content and post frequencies are resonating with similar audiences.

Within Facebook Insights or PageLever.com, you can also track how people react to different types of posts within your own Facebook page. Tag each of your own posts for the elements you've used in the content, such as questions, promotions, links, photos, videos, celebrities, specific products or storytelling, and then examine which types of content are driving the highest level of positive engagement for your organization based on your specific goals.

Twitter, Instagram and Pinterest

You can use the same technique for performance tracking on social networks like Twitter, Instagram or Pinterest as you set up on Facebook. In fact, this is a good idea because, even though the platforms are different and attract somewhat different demographics, it helps to have as much of a standard basis to compare them as is possible.

Tag each of your own posts or photos for the type of content you've used, and then look at overarching engagement trends to see which content elements drove the most positive engagement on average.

Strategic Listening Versus Tactical Listening

Listening typically falls into two distinct categories: strategic listening and tactical listening. To us, strategic listening means listening (not just hearing, but listening) in on the widest variety of social media in order to better understand our customers and prospects, and to gain insights that influence our overarching business and communication direction. Tactical listening means monitoring relevant public conversations in social media for potential issues or opportunities going on in all social media platforms 24/7 while remaining alert for potential crises to respond to and mitigate, and remaining equally alert to identify opportunities to respond to and exploit.

Before moving forward, you need to have a sense of the difference between a strategy and a tactic. A strategy is an overarching "clever plan" of action that guides us in our progress toward a specific goal, and tactics are the specific actions used to execute within that overarching plan.

Most of what we've covered in this chapter relates to strategic listening to get a better understanding of where the organization stands in order to drive both marketing and organizational-public relationship planning and to deliver results through social media. In Chapters 7 and 9, we'll take a much more tactical approach to uncover day-to-day opportunities for engagement and relationship building.

CASE STUDY 6.1—How the "World's Most Valuable
Social Network" Uses Sysomos Heartbeat to
Find Missing Children

The Missing Children Society of Canada (MCSC) is a nonprofit
organization dedicated to reuniting missing children with their
families. It works with law enforcement agencies, communities,
professional investigators and the families themselves to aid in the
search for missing children.

MCSC believed that social media's reach could give the
organization a strong new tool to help find missing children.
While MCSC had used social media for years to publicize fundraising events and corporate partnerships, it was looking for ways
to leverage social media further. In 2012, their partner Grey
Canada created the "World's Most Valuable Social Network," a
social media app designed to propagate missing child alerts to as
many people as possible.

As a social communications leader, Marketwired was a natural choice to help MCSC track the success of their initiative and
make the most of every opportunity to raise awareness about it.

Harnessing the Power of Donated Social Networks

The first 48 hours after a child goes missing are the most important—the child may still be close to home and people's memories
of seeing the child will be fresh. During this time, the child's community can be instrumental in finding him or her. The "World's
Most Valuable Social Network" allows users to "donate" their
social media accounts to alert everyone in that person's social network when a child goes missing.

This is a brand new way of using social media to help find
missing children. Users give MCSC the ability to post an alert on
their Facebook and Twitter feeds so when an AMBER alert or
other active missing child investigation takes place, MCSC does-
n't have to wait for people to share or retweet its updates—it has
instant access. People who see the alert can view information
about the missing child, sign up for the app themselves, and, most
important, report a sighting of the child to MCSC or law enforcement. Early adopters of the Most Valuable Network included

celebrities like singer Sarah McLachlan and sports announcer Rob Kerr.

With access to these donated networks, MCSC predicted that a greater number of people would see its alerts than by using its own social media outreach and advertising, but the organization needed a way to measure the app's effectiveness. It quickly found a solution. Since 2003, MCSC has relied on Marketwired to publicize its news and initiatives. In 2008, they began incorporating social media press releases into their efforts—the success of that effort led them to explore other uses of social media. After researching various social media monitoring products, the organization realized it had the best tool at its fingertips and brought in Heartbeat (powered by Sysomos) to measure the Most Valuable Network's reach and learn how to make it even better.

Making the World's Most Valuable Social Network Even More Valuable

"The real value of (Sysomos) Heartbeat is that it allows us to track impressions from the *World's Most Valuable Network* a lot more clearly than what we could with Twitter on its own. (Heartbeat) makes it easy to look for different mentions," says Chantal Bazinet, MCSC's senior communications officer. MCSC uses the *World's Most Valuable Network* to push out information that needs to be seen as soon as possible.

Heartbeat gives MCSC insight into what makes the alerts more likely to be shared quickly. For instance, MCSC started to notice that updates that contained hashtags were retweeted more, so they now include hashtags in all of their alerts.

In addition, the law enforcement agencies that MCSC partnered with wanted proof that social media outreach was having a positive effect. "Law enforcement requires us to be able to demonstrate how many people are seeing our alerts," says Chantal Bazinet. "We showed them that we have an average reach of more than 1.2 million impressions per alert sent out via the *World's Most Valuable Network*. Each alert receives over 3,000 posts and tweets and the network continues to grow with each use."

Working Toward the Goal of Reuniting All Missing Children with Their Families

MCSC uses social media for many different initiatives. It plans to continue using Heartbeat to monitor the "World's Most Valuable Network," improving its effectiveness by tuning messages and noting what helps get more sign-ups for the app. It also uses social media to publicize additional missing child cases on birthdays and anniversaries of the child's disappearance. Heartbeat tracks these posts and suggests ways to boost the number of impressions.

By using "donated" networks and tracking impressions with Heartbeat, MCSC has found a much more cost-effective and efficient way to get the message out than by using advertising and its own network. MCSC plans to continue to use Heartbeat to expand use of the app to make sure that missing children have the greatest possible chance to be found.

Reprinted with permission: Marketwired.com

❊ ❊ ❊

Making Your Practice Perfect

Exercise: Do Your Own Content Analysis

It's time to put analysis into action. Follow the steps below to do your own content analysis.

Action 1: Determine Your Sample Size

- Set up your keywords in your listening tool of choice.
- Determine the time period that you will examine.
- Go to *http://surveysystem.com/sscalc.htm* and enter the total number of posts that you want to analyze for that time period into the "Population" box. Enter your confidence level (we usually use 95%) and your confidence interval (we usually use 5). Hit "Calculate" to determine how many posts you will need to evaluate for your sample set.
- If you do not have the ability to randomly sample your posts, divide the total number of posts in your population

by the total number of posts in your sample size (e.g., 4,000 total posts divided by a sample size of 351 equals 11.4). Round down (in this case, you would tag every 11th post).

- Export your social posts to Excel. If you are using free search tools that do not allow you to export directly to Excel, search the phrase "Export RSS to Excel" on your search engine of choice for tutorials about how to get your search results into Excel.

Action 2: Determine How You Will Tag Sentiment

Scan the search results with your team, and determine whether you will tag posts based on reader influence or writer feelings. Create a basic tagging guide to outline how the team will approach tagging sentiment and key topics based on the team's listening objectives. Consider these questions:

—Are you tracking reactions to your initiatives? If so, include the basic brand initiatives that you want to keep an eye out for, and discuss what you consider to be positive, neutral or negative reactions around those initiatives.

—Are you tracking for opinions related to specific products or product attributes? What key products or product attributes should the team keep an eye out for?

—Are you tracking organization visibility in the media? If so, consider including tags such as "feature," "aside" and "comparison" and defining what types of outlets will be tagged as "key media."

—Are you tagging for customer service issues? Have you seen issues through more traditional channels that you want to track closely in social media?

—Will you track the impact of social sharing, such as linked articles, hashtags, replies and retweets?

—Are you tagging each post for the demographics of the writer? If so, what will you keep an eye out for? Gender? Media outlet category? City? State? Region?

Action 3: Tag Your Sample Set

Use your tagging guideline to tag your set of social posts for relevancy, context and sentiment. Each separate tag should be in its own column within your spreadsheet so that you can automatically add up your results. For a step-by-step guide on how to tally your results within Excel, go to *http://TheSocialCurrent.com/ resources.*

7

Finding Potential Influencers for Your Organization or Industry

---

More and more companies are realizing that the social Web is transforming how they interact with customers.

—Marcel LeBrun
CEO
Radian6

In this chapter, you will learn:

- How to use free and/or paid tools to identify outlets and individuals who may be relevant to your organization.
- How to qualify specific outlets and individuals before reaching out.

Essential Term for Chapter 7

- **Blogroll:** Bloggers often include lists of other recommended bloggers on their sites.

STEP 7—Finding Potential Influencers for Your Organization or Industry

As long as social media have been around, there have been debates over how best to identify and build relationships with potential influencers within any given category. Communicators all over the world have come under attack for being careless with their initial research and sending out spam-like emails to people who are not necessarily relevant to their messages.

If one of your listening objectives is to find out which outlets or individuals are influencing social media conversations related to your organization or industry, listen up. Whatever you do, please don't start blasting out emails to anyone you can find who has ever mentioned anything related to your industry. Do your research first.

Identifying Potential Influencers

Influencer research is not a perfect science. There are two approaches to gathering a list of people who may be influencing perspectives within your industry:

1. Keep an ongoing list of people and outlets who have talked about your industry. Read content from these people and outlets regularly, and start building relationships with them by commenting on their blogs and being a part of relevant conversations via Twitter and other relevant social platforms.
2. If you are planning to do research around a particular event in the near future, you may build a list more quickly. But, whatever you do, make sure you *read* the content from each individual to get to know the author before reaching out.

If you're starting from scratch, most professional listening tools will allow you to sort by "influence" based on some combination of estimated monthly readers, followers, comments, inbound links or other similar metrics. Other tools focus specifically on finding potential influencers based on categories and keywords. Keep an eye on our wiki at ***http://TheSocialCurrent. com/wiki*** to see details on these tools.

Don't just create an export of names from your tool of choice and start reaching out without doing your own reading and research. Again, this will require a combination of machine sorting and human analysis.

If you don't have access to paid tools to help you with your influencer research, start by searching the profiles of Twitter users to find people who are interested in your industry, then follow through to see if they have blogs or other social media platforms.

Free Tools to Search Twitter Profiles

—FollowerWonk.com
—Twellow.com

For example, Mary from Eco Redux Studio might search for people who have mentioned one of the following combinations in their Twitter profiles:

—"eco fashion"
—"green fashion"

Though the Friendlie Bank team has not specifically mentioned connecting with industry influencers in their list of business objectives, they might search for mentions of the following combinations in Twitter profiles to see what comes up:

—banking
—banks
—finance

The Mega Burger team might search for the following combinations:

—"food blogger"
—"restaurant reviews"

Steven from Hartlin Kids might search for of the following combinations:

—children health
—"childhood obesity"
—health issues
—nutrition

Finally, Amy, the marketing consultant, may look for people with one of the following combinations:

—marketing
—small business
—small businesses

Depending on the niche, you may not necessarily want to focus on building relationships with the *biggest* influencers. Marketing, for example, is a huge category, and many of the top influencers already have scores of people who are reaching out to them each day. You may have better luck focusing on more specific niches, whether by topic or location, or by focusing on people and outlets who are slightly less dominating within your category. For example, Steven may look for people within a specific geography who are influential in that area, and Amy might look for niche marketing outlets and professionals that could complement her own offerings.

Identifying Relevant Blogs

Beyond tracing Twitter profiles to blogs, there are a few additional free ways to approach searching for influential blogs in your category:

- —Blogrolls
- —BlogDash.com
- —Blogs.com curated "Top Ten" lists
- —AllTop.com
- —Google Search

Blogrolls

Popular bloggers often include blogrolls on their sites to share other blogs similar to their own. Once you've identified a blog to keep track of through Twellow.com, FollowerWonk.com or another method, check out the blogger's blogroll to see who else she recommends within the category.

BlogDash.com

BlogDash has curated a list of thousands of bloggers across more than 15 categories. A free subscription will give you access to see basic descriptions for each, along with notes about whether each author is "PR friendly" or open to receiving messages from marketers. A paid subscription allows users to engage with bloggers directly through the BlogDash dashboard.

Blogs.com "Top Ten" Lists

Blogs.com has curated hundreds of blogger top ten lists across different categories under *http://www.blogs.com/topten*. Be aware that these have been curated by individuals and will not necessarily be all-inclusive or relevant to your own objectives.

AllTop.com

Similar to Blogs.com, AllTop.com has curated lists of blogs across dozens of niche categories. The same warning applies here— know that these lists have been curated by individuals and will still require additional research on your end.

Google Search

Never underestimate the power of Google. Try a simple Google search for your category, such as:

- Best marketing blogs
- Top marketing blogs
- Must-read marketing blogs

These will usually return curated lists that others have put together of their favorite resources in any given category.

Think Outside the Box

If you're having trouble identifying people who may be influential to your industry, take a step back. Your searches may be too specific. For example, if you run a software company that has developed screen recording software, you wouldn't set out to find the top influencers in the "screen recording" category. If your category is too niche to have outlets entirely dedicated to it, make a list of target audiences and categories who may also benefit from your products or services. In the case of screen capturing software, any of the following categories may apply:

- Education
- Life hacks (tricks to save time and be more efficient)
- Advice for small businesses (use screen recording for training or marketing)
- Gamers (gamers often record themselves playing games)

If you get stuck, brainstorm as many "outside the box" categories as you can. Then select a few key audiences to focus on.

Qualifying Outlets for Relevance

As you start to collect a list of outlets that may be influencing your category, create a spreadsheet or document to keep track of the following elements, where applicable. This information will help you to prioritize which outlets to focus on more closely.

- **Outlet name:** The name of the blog or outlet.
- **Outlet URL:** The blog or outlet URL.
- **Author name(s):** The name of the author. If you are looking at an outlet with multiple authors, find the author who is most relevant to your topic based on other articles that he has written in the past.
- **Twitter handle(s):** List Twitter handles from the outlet and/or individual.
- **Twitter followers:** Though Twitter followers certainly don't equate directly to "influence," this will be one metric of many to understand who each author is and make a final decision on who to build relationships with.
- **Blog readership:** Use tools like Compete.com and Quantcast.com to estimate how many unique monthly visitors each outlet gets. Again, you will not be making your final decisions based on this metric alone. This number is simply an estimate, and there are other ways that blogs and outlets engage with their communities beyond monthly readers, such as RSS and newsletter subscribers.
- **Comments:** Read through comments to the blog or outlet. Are readers highly engaged? Keep notes about general reader engagement.
- **Google PageRank:** Use *http://www.prchecker.info* to find out the outlet's Google PageRank. PageRank tracks the relative "importance" of a site based on other sites that are linking to it.
- **Reader demographics:** Quantcast.com will estimate demographic information for the readers of sites with enough readers. Note that demographic estimations are based on a representative set of visitors and may suffer from some selection bias.
- **General notes:** Add additional qualitative comments about each outlet. Read about each author and keep track of anything that may be notable for your research.
- **Contact:** Look for contact information. This will typically come in the form of an email address or contact form on an "about" or "contact" page.

Content Relevance

We mentioned an easy search trick in Chapter 5 to use Google to find out whether any given blog or outlet has ever mentioned your organization or competitors. Let's take a look at this again.

keywords site:URL /

For example, if we want to find out whether LifeHacker.com has ever mentioned screen recording software in the past, we might do a search such as:

"screen recording" OR "screen capturing" site:http://lifehacker.com

This will return all posts that have mentioned the exact phrases "screen recording" or "screen capturing" within Life-Hacker.com. Using that same method, we could search for mentions of specific screen recording softwares:

camtasia OR screenflow OR "screen flow" site:http://lifehacker.com

This will return any specific mentions of Camtasia or Screen-Flow, two specific screen recording softwares.

You can do the same for Twitter using Twitter search (http://twitter.com/search), though you may not be able to access as much historical data using this free tool:

camtasia OR screenflow OR "screen flow" from: Lifehacker

This will return mentions of Camtasia or ScreenFlow from Twitter user @lifehacker.

Why Research Matters

Years ago, when we were reaching out to home improvement bloggers to invite them to take part in the launch of a new household cleaner, we learned a valuable lesson. We researched and read before reaching out, and when we finally did, we heard back from one blogger who mentioned that she only focused on all natural household-cleaning products. Looking back, we had missed an earlier blog post from this blogger about creating homemade all-natural cleaning products. Though we had done enough research to know that a cleaning product was relevant to this blogger, we had stopped just short of realizing that the only cleaning products that might be relevant would have been all-natural ones.

Before you reach out to anyone, read as much as you can, and use the *site:URL* search method to uncover any potential objections they may have.

If the blogger is already a huge fan of your competitor, you may be better off skipping him. If a blogger has expressed feelings that conflict with your products or services, you probably shouldn't reach out.

Do your research and get personal, and you're on your way to building successful relationships. If you blast out emails without reading first, get ready to find yourself on the next list of "PR Disasters."

CASE STUDY 7.1—Helping a U.S. Food Company to Understand What Consumers Really Want

The Challenge

Loudpixel's team of analysts was approached by a U.S. food company that was planning to completely rebrand and relaunch one of its product lines. The line's makeover included a new logo, new packaging and new marketing messages around the relaunch.

The brand team assumed that its key audience was made up of active women who would be drawn to the product line as an easy, on-the-go snack that fit in with their busy lifestyles, but before beginning the planning and design process around the relaunch, the company wanted to fully understand its core audience, including perceptions related to the brand, key competitors and the product category as a whole. They also wanted to understand motivators and detractors for buying different products within the category.

The Approach

To understand these key areas, Loudpixel exported a set of more than 35,000 social media posts about the company's brand and competitors from the listening tool Radian6. The analysts also used Loudpixel's analysis tool, Levee, to create a representative sample set and tag social media posts for relevancy, sentiment, context and demographics. The team was particularly focused on answering the following questions:

- What are the top brands being mentioned in social media around the product category?
- Demographics: who is talking about the brand, competitors and category in social media, and how do perceptions vary by gender, age and/or location?
- What does sentiment breakdown look like for each brand?
- What are the top positive and negative conversation drivers for each brand (e.g., product attributes, general brand perceptions)?
- What are the top conversation drivers in social media across the entire product category, including reactions to the following:
  ‣ Price
  ‣ Product attributes (e.g., ingredients, flavors offered, taste, etc.)
  ‣ Branding/packaging
  ‣ Brand initiatives/marketing
  ‣ Motivations for consuming the products (nutrition/ wellness, taste, brand image, sharing with friends in social situations, etc.)
  ‣ Associations with celebrities/pop culture
- Who are the top social and mainstream media influencers related to the products and category as a whole? Which outlets are being referenced the most?

After analyzing the social media posts, Loudpixel's analysts created a report to summarize findings for the brand team, including the following key insights:

- While the company had assumed that the product market was completely female dominated, social research revealed that men were just as likely to discuss and consume the product as the female audience.
- While the company had assumed that the product was perceived as a general lifestyle product (easy to consume on the go), conversations across the entire category were actu-

ally largely driven by references to health, nutrition and ingredients.

The Results

These overarching insights led the brand team to take a few new approaches that they had not previously considered:

- While the team had previously been considering packaging that would appeal solely to a female audience, they ended up with a design that would appeal to both men and women.
- The team decided to put greater emphasis on the fact that their products are all natural, a topic that was clearly important to their core audience.
- The team used the list of media influencers—sites that were being referenced the most in relation to the product category—as a starting point to build relationships with bloggers and journalists in preparation for the relaunch. They were particularly keen on nutrition and fitness outlets that could align with health and nutrition messaging.

CASE STUDY 7.2—A New Online Sports Video Channel Learns How to Create Engaging Content and Promote Its Launch to Social Influencers

The Challenge

A media company was in the early stages of planning to launch a new online golf video channel when it approached Loudpixel to help understand the nature of existing social media conversations related to golf and sports. Before investing in particular show concepts, the team needed to understand what topics and types of content would resonate with audiences and drive the highest online engagement. They also wanted to know which brands were already associated with golf that could benefit from engaging with the new channel as sponsors and partners. Finally, the team wanted to know who was already influencing the golf community online so that they could look for opportunities to build relationships to promote the new channel when it was ready to launch.

The Approach

Loudpixel's analysts downloaded a set of 300 social media posts from the listening tool Radian6. The posts were selected based on the most engagement in four areas:

- Most viewed videos and photos related to golf
- Most unique comments to blog and mainstream news posts
- Most Twitter followers
- Most posts to forum threads

The team imported the posts into Loudpixel's content analysis tool, Levee, and tagged them for relevancy, sentiment and context. The analysis was particularly focused on tagging the posts for the following areas:

- Elements of highly engaged social content (e.g., celebrity involvement, how-to tips, humor, current events, etc.)
- Particular celebrity names (Who is the most likely to be associated with highly engaged posts about golf? Are popular celebrities associated with golf more likely to be professional golfers or other celebrities?)
- Branded content versus unbranded content

Beyond this, the Loudpixel team identified specific social media influencers who were driving the highest volume of conversations in the following categories:

- Professional golfers
- Popular Twitter users who golf
- Forums
- Blogs
- Videos

The Results

Based on this analysis, the team was able to identify the top elements that drove highly engaged social media posts related to golf. This information was used to drive the content mix for the new channel.

By identifying brands that were creating engaging content related to golf, the team was able to:

- Identify brands that could be potential partners or advertisers for the new channel.

- Identify the elements of highly engaging branded content around golf to understand what types of branded content are the most likely to create successful partnerships with brands.

Beyond this, by identifying the top influencers in social media related to golf, the team was able to identify a list of individuals and outlets to reach out to and partner with when it came time to promote the new channel.

Ultimately, Loudpixel's research helped the media company develop a content strategy, discover new brand partnerships and uncover relationships and partnerships with influencers to help promote the launch of the channel.

✵ ✵ ✵

Making Your Practice Perfect

Exercise: Create a Spreadsheet of Potential Relationships

It's time to put these steps into action for yourself. Create a spreadsheet of at least 10 potential people or outlets to start building relationships with. Include the following columns in your spreadsheet to compare each outlet:

- Outlet name
- Outlet URL
- Author Name(s)
- Twitter handle(s)
- Twitter followers
- Blog readership
- Comments
- Google PageRank
- Reader demographics
- General notes
- Contact

Start by reading these blogs and outlets regularly, leaving comments when appropriate and engaging on Twitter. Plan to update and grow this list over time.

8

Presenting Your Findings

---

*Figures often beguile me, particularly when I have
the arranging of them myself; in which case the remark
attributed to Disraeli would often apply with justice
and force: 'There are three kinds of lies:
lies, damned lies and statistics.'*

—Mark Twain

In this chapter, you will learn:

- How to present your data to the organization in a consistent, concise way.
- How to present your findings to different audiences within the organization.

Essential Term for Chapter 8

- **Sources and Methods Transparency Table:** A table used to display specific methods used to gather social media research findings.

STEP 8—Presenting Your Findings

After diving into social media content analysis, you're likely overflowing with data and findings. Now it's time to select and present the findings that matter the most. Rather than running the risk of overwhelming your teammates with every possible statistic, focus on data and findings that tie back to your specific objectives—findings that answer specific questions and that lead to possible action within the organization.

Data Can Lie

You want to avoid information overload while presenting your findings, but you also want to make sure that you're telling the whole story. For example, take a look at the pie chart below.

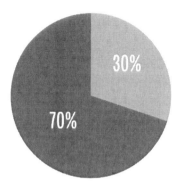

Sentiment

Let's say that this sentiment chart represents that 70% of posts are positive and 30% are neutral. How many posts were there? This chart might represent ten posts or it might represent ten thousand. Without this context, you're missing part of the story.

Use Appropriate Charts

Make sure that you are using the correct charts to display your data. For example, see if you can figure out what might be wrong with the example below.

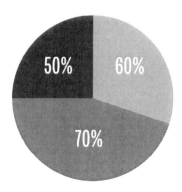

The pie chart has three figures that add up to more than 100%. While it is possible to have data sets that add up to more than 100%, you can't have more than 100% of a pie. So the principle here is that you can only use pie charts for data sets with no overlaps, where the percentages add up to exactly 100%. If there is overlap in your data points that will cause your percentages to exceed 100%, use bar charts to convey your information.

One example of a situation in which you'll have data points that add up to more than 100%, or overlaps, is in contextual data reporting on social media conversations. In these cases, each post may have multiple tags used for sorting. A single comment may be recorded and reported falling into both a "brand message" and an "advertising" category, for example. These data points would be better presented with exact numbers, as in the horizontal bar chart below.

Take a look at the next example. In this case, the charts are correct, but they're confusing. There are simpler ways display these data points.

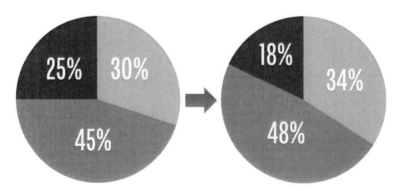

These pie charts force readers to go back and forth to try to figure out the changes displayed from one chart to the next. These data points would be easier to understand in simple table form.

	Q1	Q2	CHANGE
DATA POINT 1	30%	34%	+4%
DATA POINT 2	45%	48%	+3%
DATA POINT 3	25%	18%	-7%

Chart Colors

When showing charts for sentiment in color, stick to this standard color scheme:

- **Green:** Positive
- **Red:** Negative
- **Blue:** Neutral

Don't try to spice up your charts by using other colors to represent these three sentiment types. You will only confuse your readers.

Tips for Effective Reporting

Know Your Audience

When creating a report to show your findings, first get a clear understanding of your audience. Will the principal viewers of the data and charts be an internal team that will be expected to take direct action on the findings? Will the charts be presented to the company's CEO? These two "audiences" are different and will probably require a different presentation of the data. The team will probably require detailed findings, while the CEO more often than not will prefer a broad overview of findings such as would be presented in an executive summary. The principle here is that if your data are going to be of interest to different audiences, it's most likely that you will need to create separate reports or versions that address the specific needs of each.

Be Consistent

When your team sets out to create reports that track progress for the organization, use the benchmark report as a template. Include metrics based on specific objectives, and report on these metrics in every report.

We've seen companies create two separate reports for the same organization, and the reports look nothing alike and convey information on completely different metrics. Such inconsistency will cause the reports to be devalued. Remember this: When you are attempting to demonstrate performance that you have tracked over time, it's essential that you compare "apples to apples."

Be Transparent with Your Sources and Methods

The concept of transparency suggests functioning in such a way as to allow light to shine so that the inner workings will be clearly visible to the naked eye.

In 2012, the Coalition for PR Research Standards published a "Sources and Methods Transparency Table" to be included within all PR and social media reports. This table shows full transparency into the methods used to collect and analyze the data within the report.

Include the chart below, or create your own version of the chart, to clearly show how you arrived at your findings within the report.

Sources and Methods Transparency Table	
Timeframe Analyzed	
Research Leads	
Channels Analyzed	
Data/Content Sources	
Analysis Depth	☐ Automated ☐ Manual ☐ Hybrid ☐ All Content Reviewed ☐ Rep. Sample
Source Languages	
Sentiment Coding	☐ Automated ☐ Manual ☐ Hybrid ☐ Manual Sampling: _____ ☐ 3-pt scale ☐ 5-pt scale ☐ Other scale ☐ At entity level ☐ Paragraph/doc level
Spam/Bot Filtering	☐ Automated ☐ Manual ☐ Hybrid ☐ Includes news releases
Metrics Calculation and Sources	
Reach	
Engagement	
Influence	
Opinion/Advocacy	
Proprietary Methods	
Search Parameters	

Source: #SMMStandards (www.smmstandards.org)

Here's a sample of a sources and methods transparency table with details included:

Sources and Methods Transparency Table	
Timeframe Analyzed	September 1 - December 31, 2013
Research Leads	Allie Siarto, Loudpixel Inc.
Channels Analyzed	Blogs, comments, Twitter, forums, videos, images, public Facebook posts, mainstream news
Data/Content Sources	Radian6, PageLever.com, PeekAnalytics
Analysis Depth	☐ Automated ☐ Manual ☐ Hybrid ☐ All Content Reviewed ■ Rep. Sample
Source Languages	English
Sentiment Coding	☐ Automated ☐ Manual ☐ Hybrid ☐ Manual Sampling: _____ ■ 3-pt scale ☐ 5-pt scale ☐ Other scale ☐ At entity level ☐ Paragraph/doc level
Spam/Bot Filtering	☐ Automated ☐ Manual ■ Hybrid ☐ Includes news releases
Metrics Calculation and Sources	
Potential Reach	Daily unique visitors for specific URLs via Quantcast.com (no multipliers), aggregate Twitter followers for all posts that mentioned the brand (via Radian6) and unique Facebook page visits (via PageLever)
Engagement	Social posts and Facebook likes, comments, clicks, views or plays
Influence	Determined by an analyst based on readership, comments, retweets and relevancy
Opinion/Advocacy	Human reading and coding
Proprietary Methods	Loudpixel used a proprietary method for calculating the quarter index score (see index section for details)
Search Parameters	A spreadsheet of all specific keywords is available upon request

Your formatting doesn't necessarily have to follow this chart format directly, as long as you have a page dedicated to openly sharing the details of your research. The idea is that another member on your team could look at your methods and replicate them in a follow- up report.

In fact, a bulleted list may offer you more flexibility to share the specific details of your own research. Here's an example of a sources and methods transparency table from a Loudpixel report:

- **Timeframe Analyzed:** September 1–December 31, 2013
- **Research Leads:** Allie Siarto, Lesley Smith, Loudpixel Inc.

- **Channels Analyzed:** Blogs, comments, Twitter, forums, videos, images, public Facebook posts, mainstream news
- **Data/Content Sources:** Radian6, PageLever, PeekAnalytics
- **Analysis Depth:** Representative sample set (95% confidence level, confidence interval of 5)
- **Search Language:** English
- **Sentiment Coding:** 4-pt scale (positive, neutral, negative, irrelevant), hand tagged based on representative sample
- **Spam/Bot Filtering:** Manual filtering based on representative sample
- **Metrics Calculation:**
  - ▸ **Post Volume:** Total relevant posts across blogs, comments, Twitter, Friendfeed, forums, videos, images, mainstream news and comments to admin posts on the brand Facebook page(s)
  - ▸ **Potential Twitter Reach:** Aggregate Twitter followers for all posts that mentioned the brand (via Radian6)
  - ▸ **Engagement:** Social posts (see post volume above) and Facebook likes, comments, clicks, views or plays
  - ▸ **Influence:** Determined by an analyst based on readership, comments, retweets and relevancy
  - ▸ **Search Parameters:** A spreadsheet of all keywords is available upon request—keywords are updated regularly to ensure relevancy
- **Additional Notes:** This list is provided in an effort to comply with the new Coalition for Public Relations research standards.

If you work on a team, transparency and consistency are the keys to successful reporting. Get these details in place with the first report to avoid confusion later on.

CASE STUDY 8.1—Loudpixel Creates Infographics Around Trending Topics in Social Media to Position Itself as a Market Leader

The Challenge

In 2011, the Loudpixel team recognized that mainstream media outlets were beginning to publish tweets and social media trends as news stories. In the world of 24/7 news, the media now follows a cycle of reporting on news, tracking social media trends in response to the news and then reporting back on how people are reacting to the stories.

Loudpixel wanted to find a way to capitalize on this news cycle and position itself as an expert in the media by creating relevant content that journalists could use in their stories.

The Approach

The Loudpixel team began keeping an eye out for hot topics in the news that were gaining large responses in social media. As hot topics were identified, the team analyzed basic quantitative information around the topics in social media and presented the findings through infographics. The infographics were published to the Loudpixel blog.

Examples include:
Netflix and Qwikster Split, 2011:

By the Numbers   ☐ **loudpixel** Infographics
Social Media Conversations Related to Netflix/Qwikster Split

96 — Number of posts per minute from September 19-20, 2011

746 — Percent increase in conversation related to Netflix from September 18 to September 19

6,141 — References to The Oatmeal comic mocking the decision: http://theoatmeal.com/comics/netflix

14,535 — Number of posts referencing price from September 19-20, 2011

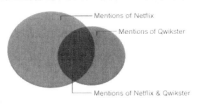

Mentions of Netflix
Mentions of Qwikster
Mentions of Netflix & Qwikster

Most common misspellings of Qwikster:
Quickster 1,935 posts   **Qwickster** 1,278 posts

and SOPA (Stop Online Piracy Act), 2012:

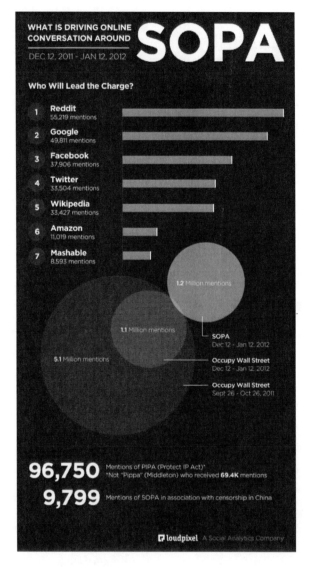

The Results

By presenting social media research findings in a creative way, Loudpixel was able capture the attention of larger media outlets who approached the company about media partnerships to create ongoing infographics. This allowed Loudpixel to get the company name in front of a broader audience on a consistent basis. On top of this, links back to the Loudpixel website from large media organizations increased the company's search rankings, which led to an increase in inbound leads for new business.

✻ ✻ ✻

Making Your Practice Perfect

Exercise: Outline Your Report

Let's take action. Follow the steps below:

- Determine the audience for your report.
- Go through the results of your social content analysis to determine which findings will be the most relevant and actionable for this audience based on your listening objectives.
- Outline the graphs that you will show in the final report, along with supporting details, such as specific social post examples and notes that support your findings.
- Create a "Sources and Methods Transparency Table" to outline how you arrived at your results.

9

Using Benchmark Reporting to Identify Potential Opportunities and Threats

A pessimist sees the difficulty in every opportunity; an optimist sees the opportunity in every difficulty.

Winston Churchill

In this chapter, you will learn:

- How to use your benchmark research to set up specific keyword alerts.
- How to set up a workflow to monitor social conversations on a daily basis.

Essential Terms for Chapter 9

- **Alert Keywords:** Keywords used to monitor specific potential issues in social media on a day-to-day-basis.
- **Response Flow Chart:** A diagram that walks team members through a plan of action to respond to individual social media posts on a day-to-day basis.
- **Response Plan:** A plan of action that is put together to guide a team on how to respond to individual social media posts on a day-to-day basis.

STEP 9—Using Benchmark Reporting to Identify Potential Opportunities and Threats

Whenever an organization comes to us to put together a monitoring program, we always recommend that they start with a deeper dive analysis first. This analysis will help you to better understand the types of topics your audience really talks about to better outline the topics that present potential issues. If you haven't already, go back to Chapter 6 to understand how to do your benchmark conversation analysis.

Tracking Potential Customer Service Issues

Like it or not, social media are starting to become go-to channels for customer service questions and complaints. We've seen measurable decreases in traditional customer service inquiries such as phone and email with our clients over the past few years. This is very likely driven by the ease of taking to the Web to post questions and complaints publicly through social media. In many cases, we suspect that this increase is driven more by retaliation than it is by a sense that their complaint will be rectified.

In Chapter 5, we outlined keywords to track social conversations related to your organization, competitors and industry. Now it's time to overlay subcategories related to potential issues and alerts.

If you already have a customer service department, start there. Meet with the customer service team to gather details around common customer service requests and complaints through more traditional channels that could also be tracked through social media listening. Next, evaluate any specific questions or negative conversation drivers that came up during your benchmark report.

Once you've created a list of potential questions and issues, it's time to set up your alert keywords. Once again, use *http://twitter.com/search* to test out your keywords.

Eco Redux Studio Potential Alert Keywords

Mary at Eco Redux Studio sits down with her team to create a list of keywords to start tracking around her company.
Examples include:

- boycott
- boycotting
- disappointed
- disappointing

- "falling apart"
- greenwash
- "green wash"
- greenwashing
- "green washing"
- hate
- horrible
- "never again"
- management
- manager
- offensive
- return
- returns
- quality
- service
- sucks
- sue
- sued
- suing
- terrible

Friendlie Bank Potential Alert Keywords

The Friendlie Bank team sits down to create a list of keywords to start tracking for potential issues:

Examples include:

- boycott
- boycotting
- closing AND account
- disappointed
- disappointing
- "done with"
- "done w/"
- fraud
- fraudulent
- hate
- horrible
- jipped
- leaving
- "never again"
- management

- manager
- offensive
- "screw Friendlie Bank"
- service
- sucks
- sue
- sued
- suing
- terrible

Mega Burger Potential Alert Keywords

Based on initial social media analysis and historical customer service inquiries via traditional channels, Mega Burger creates a list of keywords to be tracked. These keywords will be overlayed with the more general keywords that track Mega Burger as a whole.

Examples include:

- awful
- boycott
- boycotting
- disappointed
- disappointing
- disgusting
- "eat this not that"
- eatthisnotthat
- "food poisoning"
- foodpoisoning
- "food poison"
- foodpoison
- gross
- hate
- horrible
- "in my food"
- "never again"
- management
- manager
- server
- service
- sick
- sucks

- sue
- sued
- suing
- terrible
- wait
- waited
- waiting
- waiter
- waitress

Hartlin Kids Potential Alert Keywords

Steven's team sits down to create a list of keywords to start tracking for potential issues.
   Examples include:

- boycott
- boycotting
- disappointed
- disappointing
- fraud
- fraudulent
- hate
- horrible
- irresponsible
- management
- manager
- offensive
- scam
- scamming
- service
- sucks

Amy Sanders Potential Alert Keywords

Because Amy, the marketing consultant, is largely concerned with her own reputation, and because her own name will be easy to track, her alert keywords will be based around general mentions of her name.
   Examples include:

- "Amy Sanders"
- amysanders
- amysandersmarketing.com

These lists will serve as a starting point, but be sure to check and update your list regularly to include additional relevant keywords and exclude keywords that drive irrelevant posts.

Also be aware that even with keyword alerts, your team will still need to read through posts to identify which posts should be responded to. It's very likely that some of these alert keywords will actually return positive responses. Examples include:

- Shout out to our excellent **server** at Mega Burger
- **Sue** and I are eating at Mega Burger for lunch today. Can't **wait!**
- I'm craving Mega Burger something **awful**.

Your team will have to work together to determine which keyword qualifiers to use to find the right balance between pulling in posts related to potential issues and excluding posts that may not be relevant. Ultimately, it will still take time each day to sort through all alerts to find the posts that require action.

Organic Posts Versus Direct Responses

When it comes to monitoring issues and opportunities, your workflow will likely be broken into two separate areas:

- Organic posts that do not address your organization's Twitter handle directly or take place within your organization's own properties.
- Direct responses or responses within your organization's own properties (e.g., Twitter replies, Facebook wall, etc.).

Organizations will almost always start in the former of these categories before they have a response plan in place, but we've found from our own experience that the longer an organization has its own social presence and the more often the team responds to organic posts, the more likely the general audience is to shift toward addressing the organization directly through Twitter replies and posts within specific organization-run platforms.

Still, the workflow for identifying organic posts versus direct responses will be different. If your team is monitoring all responses to and within your own platforms, you will quickly be able to identify any questions or complaints that are being directed at the organization. The organic posts, on the other hand, will still need to be sought out through keyword searches.

Using Automated Analysis to Identify Day-to-Day Trends

In Chapter 6, we talked about the advantages and disadvantages of automated analysis versus human analysis. When it comes to the day-to-day tracking of potential issues and opportunities, timeliness is often more important than accuracy, which means that automated analysis may provide a useful starting point for identifying trends in real time.

For example, a conversation cloud may not provide much insight on most days, but if you suddenly see an unusual word pop up in your cloud while monitoring, it will be worth looking into the cause behind this new trend.

Identifying Potential Opportunities

If you are already tracking outlets and individuals who may be influential to your category, it will be easy to spot new stories from these specific outlets that present opportunities. Beyond this, there are a few other ways to use social media listening to identify opportunities.

1. Identify an industry or pop culture trend that could drive a story or initiative related to your organization.

Again, automated analysis such as tag clouds and keyword trends may prove useful to identifying real-time conversation spikes around new topics or stories that could provide opportunities for your organization.

For example, one of Friendlie Bank's core objectives is to identify opportunities that emerge in social media that can be used to tell a positive story about Friendlie Bank on an ongoing basis. The team might use a daily monitoring tool like Radian6 or Sysomos to keep an eye out for trending keywords or seasonal stories around topics related to personal or business finance. As trends are uncovered, the team may have opportunities to contribute expert content or interviews to go along with the emerging hot topics. For example, they might see an uptick in conversations around student loans as students prepare to head off to college, which might lead to an expert interview or other content around this topic.

In the same way, Steven's team at Hartlin Kids is keeping a close eye on all posts related to children and obesity, exercise and nutrition. If a new story starts to trend around one of these topics, Steven's team may have an opportunity to create its own expert content or present its own story to take advantage of the increased interest around the given topic.

2. Identify new outlets or individuals who are starting to talk about your organization or category.

You may already have a list of outlets that are driving conversations around your organization or category, but the social web is always moving and changing. New influencers are bubbling up all the time, so it is important to keep an eye out and update your list on an ongoing basis. You may also find a real-time opportunity to engage or reach out to an influencer based on a new story that is relevant to your own messaging.

For example, Eco Redux Studio, Mega Burger, Hartlin Kids and Amy, the marketing consultant, all have objectives based around determining which outlets and individuals are driving conversations in social media around their categories in order to build relationships that will help drive awareness around their companies. Stories and conversations in social media are constantly flowing and evolving, so the teams will need to keep a constant eye out for new influencers to add to their lists. This should become a regular part of daily social media monitoring.

Creating a Response Plan

In order to respond to potential issues and opportunities before they become old news (or even worse—before they blow up into larger issues), your team must have a response plan in place. Your response plan will be broken out into a six-step process:

1. Identify potential scenarios for response.
2. Identify appropriate responses for each scenario.
3. Determine the voice of the brand.
4. Work with the legal department to craft pre-written responses where necessary.
5. Create a response flow chart.
6. Determine how often you will monitor social conversations.

1. Identify Potential Scenarios for Response

We've found that response scenarios typically fall into one of five general categories:

1. **Influencer opportunity:** An influencer writes about the organization or general category, presenting an opportunity for engagement.
2. **Trending opportunity:** A story is trending that the organization could potentially tie its name to or create content around.
3. **Potential threat to the organization's reputation:** A post or story mentions an experience or fact related to the organization that could negatively influence perceptions related to the brand. It's important to note whether a negative post is based on fact or opinion. If it is simply an opinion, and it is not trending, it may not be worth responding. If the person posting the story has the facts wrong, your team may want to correct the facts.
4. **Customer service issues:** These could be customer questions or issues with the organization's products or services.
5. **Positive customer experience:** If a customer expresses an overwhelmingly positive experience with your company, you may have an opportunity to respond to further engage and build a relationship with that customer. The ability to respond to these experiences and make them a priority will vary greatly from one company to the next.

2. Identify Appropriate Responses for Each Scenario

Use your benchmark report to identify sample posts that could fit into each scenario type, and determine whether you have more specific scenarios based on your own unique category, products or services. If you can't find any real world examples based on initial listening for your own organization, expand your search to your competitors to see if you can get a feel for the types of posts that could be coming your way in the future.

Once you have identified these categories, determine how the team will respond and, more importantly, *who* will respond. Will the same people who monitor posts be the ones to respond, or will they send the posts on to someone else in the organization to respond? Will the same team members track organic posts as those who monitor direct responses on Twitter and within branded platforms like the organization's Facebook or Pinterest page? You don't need to have pre-written responses for every last scenario, but know who on your team will be empowered to respond and who will be looped in if an issue has potential to escalate.

In the case of customer service issues, this may be as simple as having basic information available to the team member who is managing responses for each platform and determining when to direct customers to a more traditional customer service channel. For example, if the response requires the customer to share personal information, your team might advise her to call the company directly. If, however, the customer is simply wondering where to locate a specific product, a team member can share this information openly.

Know that in most cases, it's simply not possible to respond to every single post about your organization, so it is just as important to determine what you will *not* respond to as what you will. For example, smaller companies may have an easier time responding to customers who have mentioned highly positive experiences with the company, while larger companies may only be able to respond to highly positive experiences from "influential" customers, based on a threshold determined by the team. There is no single response plan that will fit with every organization.

3. Determine the Voice of the Brand

If you are a small company and you are the only one responding to customers through social media, it will be very easy to maintain a consistent brand voice. If, however, you have a team working on social media monitoring and engagement, you may need to create a consistent "brand voice" to be used by all team members. Consider putting together a guide, similar to a style guide, to outline the personality of the brand and sample responses to help the team maintain consistency.

4. Work With the Legal Department to Craft Pre-written Responses Where Necessary

If your legal team is concerned about how you will respond to specific customer questions, go through your list of potential scenarios and come up with a list of specific questions or comments that might require response. Work with your legal team to craft specific responses that can be pre-approved so that the team is able to reply in real time rather than having to wait days for legal approval when questions do come up. You won't be able to anticipate every last question, but keep a running list and update it as new questions come up.

5. Create a Response Flow Chart

Your list of potential scenarios and basic responses may be enough to get started, but many organizations find it helpful to create a flow chart for the team to work through to help the decision making process.

We use a flagging system for the organizations we work with. We have a dedicated team that monitors organic conversations (those that are not directed at the organization's Twitter handle or posted within one of its social properties). When the team identifies potential issues or opportunities, they submit tickets to the appropriate team members to follow up.

- **Green Flag:** Potential opportunity
- **Yellow Flag:** Negative customer experience or potential threat
- **Red Flag:** Trending threat

On the next page is a basic example of a flow chart where the monitoring team is sending posts to other team members for response. You can use this as a basis to create your own specific flow chart, or create your own from scratch with more specific details for how to respond.

6. Determine How Often You Will Monitor Social Conversations

Next, determine how you will staff social media monitoring. For a smaller company, you might push all posts that match your alert keywords to email, keep an eye on direct Twitter responses and only check in on larger trends once or twice a day. Or you might set up a separate monitor at your workspace to keep a casual eye on opportunities and responses in real time while you work on other things throughout the day.

For a larger organization with a higher volume of social conversations, you might decide to staff a dedicated team to keep an eye on all posts in real time. By starting with a benchmark report, your team will be better prepared to make a decision on how to staff monitoring based on conversation volume and context.

You also need to determine whether you will staff team members to track and respond to conversations outside of normal

Social Media Response Chart

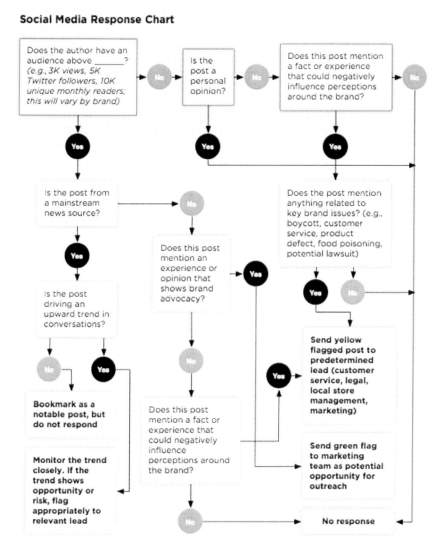

business hours. Social media doesn't stop after the work day ends, as many brands have learned the hard way.

Don't Sound the Alarm Bells Right Away

When monitoring social media posts on an ongoing basis, it's natural to have gut reactions based on the context and sentiment of just a few individual posts, but gut feelings can often be misleading. A few sample posts may be meaningless in relation to larger trends. That is to say, if one person tweets that Mega Burger needs to change the recipe for its Gigantaburger, the team may note it, but that doesn't mean they should go and report to management that customers in general are unhappy with the Gigantaburger because one person asked for a change. The team needs to evaluate the larger conversation trend and overlay this information with additional consumer research before making a decision.

For example, we saw a spike in tweets one day related to boycotting a brand that we work with. It's very common to see threats of boycotts these days for everything from advertising on the "wrong" show to creating messaging that doesn't resonate with everyone. Our guts may have told us to sound the alarm bells and go into full blown crisis mode, but on closer examination, this "trend" actually made up less than 0.4% of total conversations about the brand. Had we reacted too quickly, we may have brought unwanted attention to the other 99.6% of our audience.

Extra Point: Free Tools for Small Business Monitoring

If you're working on a limited budget, there are a few free tools that you can use to aggregate listening results from across different sources and media types. Again, check out a list of our favorite free social media monitoring and analytics tools in Chapter 4.

HootSuite offers a free way to monitor posts from sources like Twitter, blogs, forums and others. If you're using HootSuite's free version (available at http://hootsuite.com), follow the tutorial videos to set up tabs to track Twitter and your own social platforms, and then install the "RSS Reader" app to track additional RSS feeds. For example, go to *http://google.com/blogsearch* and enter a search using Boolean logic, then scroll down to the bottom of the page and select "RSS." Enter this RSS URL into HootSuite's RSS reader. HootSuite will allow you to sort feeds into separate groups as well, so take the time to organize sets of feeds based on the categories that you want to track.

———

CASE STUDY 9.1—Omnigon Communications and Comedy Central Team Up To Make the Charlie Sheen Roast a Social Event

Comedy Central

Comedy Central is an American television channel specializing in comedic programming, and Omnigon is a team of creative technologists that deliver award winning visual, software and infrastructure solutions. Together, they collaborated to make the televised Charlie Sheen Roast an interactive experience for fans by turning social media into engaging visualizations to extend the conversation beyond the event itself.

The Challenge

Omnigon is a team of creative technologists that deliver award winning visual, software and infrastructure solutions. They have been capturing conversations on the social web around events like the Daytona 500, the NBA draft, and the US Open by turning them into visualizations that give meaning to the conversations on the social web and give fans the chance to engage.

"We understand that fans want the chance to share their ideas, feedback and comments with their friends and followers on social channels like Twitter and Facebook," David Nugent, SVP, Business Development of Omnigon explains. "So when we were approached about the Charlie Sheen Roast by Comedy Central, we knew that there would be a huge volume of conversations on the social web and we wanted to help visualize and share them with viewers."

"The Charlie Sheen Roast is one of our biggest events of the year and we wanted to do something big and cool with it," said Steve Grimes, Comedy Central's Senior Vice President of Digital Media. "We looked at how do we create a companion device that will—from a user's point of view—allow them to see what is going on, share moments and talk."

The Approach

Omnigon collects social data in real time via the (Radian 6) Salesforce Marketing Cloud from channels like Twitter. Using this information, they created a dashboard that gave viewers the chance to interact and engage with other viewers during the roast. The dashboard provides the ability to contribute to the social conversation directly from the Sheen Roast via an integrated Twitter feed. The "Share the Burn" feature let users move along a timeline to the roast moments they liked best and share these with their friends and followers.

The dashboard also included the "Hot on Twitter" section, which allowed for engagement with the conversations on Sheen and the roasters. The face of each person on stage was displayed, with the size of the head growing and shrinking with his or her popularity. Then by clicking on the image of the roaster, users were able to open up a stream of social conversations about the person, and fans could actually join the conversations right there, without ever leaving the page.

The Results

The Charlie Sheen Roast was one of the most watched events in Comedy Central history, with over 6.4 million viewers. By bringing the conversations from the social web to the fans in the interactive dashboard, Omnigon helped make the roast a truly social event.

"The results were fantastic. We were able to capture the total volume of Tweets during the roast and break them down into five-minute time increments. Over the course of the two airings of the show, over 300,000 Tweets were fed into the Omnigon dashboard and another 200,000 came in following the shows," says Nugent.

Omnigon is using the social web to transform the way fans watch television, and bringing the voice of the fans to some of television's biggest events.

Reprinted with permission: Salesforcemarketingcloud.com
Source: Salesforce Marketing Cloud, Case Studies
(www.salesforcemarketingcloud.com)

CASE STUDY 9.2—The Chicago Cubs Launch a Social Media Monitoring Program to Engage with Fans

The Challenge

Before the 2010 season, the Chicago Cubs were present on social media through accounts managed by Major League Baseball, however they were not engaging with fans sending questions and comments to the team. Kevin Saghy joined the communications team as a public relations and marketing specialist that year and led the organization's plan to overhaul the Cubs' social media outlets (which were controlled by MLB at the time). The team set out to grow their online following and monitor and respond to sports fans eager to engage with the club.

The Approach

The Cubs soon created a front office Twitter account, @CubsInsider, to offer fans an opportunity to engage directly with the team. Beyond basic interactions and acknowledgements toward fans who mentioned the Cubs, the team looked for new opportunities to engage and delight fans with unique experiences. This included giveaways, surprise gifts for first-time game attendees, care packages delivered through the mail, seat upgrades and social media events that allowed team officials to meet with followers and bloggers in person.

The Results

In 2012, Major League Baseball approached Kevin's team about combining @CubsInsider with the @Cubs Twitter handle. Before the team assumed primary control of @Cubs, the account had gained a net average of roughly 75 new followers per day. Once the front office implemented its personal engagement strategy on the account, average fan growth jumped to 333 net new followers per day (a 344% increase). The Twitter handle now receives anywhere from 400 to 3,000+ mentions each day, and the team continues to actively respond to many of them. As the communications team's resources have expanded, so too has the quality and quantity of the surprise personal interactions with fans. Hashtags now appear on Cubs game tickets, and followers are rewarded for using them "in game." Followers of the team frequently win Cubs merchandise, game-used and autographed memorabilia, and personal experiences at the ballpark. These activities have attracted local and national media attention, including placement on the front page of the Sports Sunday section of *The New York Times* in an Associated Press article titled "Social Networking Comes to the Ballpark." The personal approach is paying off financially as well. Kevin and his team received a note from a fan that invested in season tickets, specifically citing the positive experiences he had with the Cubs on social media.

CASE STUDY 9.3—Loudpixel Works with a Global Brand to Identify Trending Topics for On-the-Fly Media Opportunities

The Challenge

Loudpixel was approached by a global brand that recognized that the pace of the news cycle was becoming much faster with the social web. The brand team asked the Loudpixel team to help them set up a program to tap into day-to-day trends around their industry and help them identify conversation topics where the brand could insert itself as an expert and grow its share of voice in social and mainstream news among its product category.

The Approach

Loudpixel worked with the company to set up a daily listening program using the social media monitoring tool Radian6. The team started with a benchmark analysis of social and mainstream articles to understand how the brand was already being perceived within its category. Once brand perceptions and hot topics within the category were identified, these topics became the building blocks for daily listening.

Loudpixel broke out keyword alerts around topics that were already popular within the product category to keep a close eye on how these topics impacted conversations around the category over time. From there, the team started tracking general daily conversations and trending topics for potential opportunities. Each morning, the Loudpixel team identified a set of specific popular topics that the brand could tie itself to and submitted the list to the brand's public relations team that was ready to create expert content and secure interviews around relevant topics.

The Results

By monitoring for daily trends and opportunities, the brand was able to react more quickly to ongoing media opportunities and grow its mainstream and social media presence by tying itself to topics that readers were particularly interested in reading about and sharing.

✣ ✣ ✣

Making Your Practice Perfect

Exercise: Create a Response Workflow

It's time to take action. Follow the steps below:

- Identify potential scenarios that you want to track and create your initial alert keyword list.
- Identify appropriate responses for each potential scenario.
- Determine the voice of your brand.
- If necessary, work with your legal department to craft prewritten responses around particular issues.
- Outline sample scenarios with details about how your team will respond, or create a detailed response flow chart to guide your team.
- Determine how often your team will monitor social conversations.

Conclusion

People will use social networks to talk about you,
your brand and your products,
whether you choose to participate or not.

—Julie Blakley
Digital Marketing Manager
Postano

Recognize That Listening Is a Continuous Process

Marketing communications and public relations once operated largely in the world of *campaigns*. Each campaign was planned to have a beginning and an end, and by virtue of that concept of a campaign, the budget for each campaign was a fixed amount of funding. The budget was perceived to have a beginning and an end as well. Social media have turned the concept of campaigns upside down, in part because social media, like the monitoring and analysis you are learning to do, is a continuous process. Consider this as you set your social listening budget.

Your monitoring and analysis budget should be set up to accommodate an ongoing process. Also consider how the concept of listening might change from one year to the next. As we mentioned earlier, we've seen the volume of social media posts increase by 5 to 15 times across brands that we've tracked in just three years. And with the ever-growing interest in social media, this trend will only go up.

Evaluate your listening tools and staffing plan regularly to make sure that they align with the needs of the organization, and audit your keywords on an ongoing basis to make sure that you continue to pull in relevant social posts. If your team adds a new product, tag line, website, hashtag or anything else that may change how people talk about your organization, make sure that this is reflected in your keywords.

The success of your listening program depends on your commitment to stay actively involved in it. While this can present some challenges along the way, the insights, opportunities and connections that can come from a commitment to listening will be well worth the effort. Remember, communication is a two-way street. The thing that distinguishes communication from speaking is, in fact, listening.

Listening is not synonymous with hearing. Hearing is a physiological process of detecting some kind of sound. Listening is differentiated by virtue of the implication that when we listen, we learn. When we listen, the information that we take in has some effect on our behavior.

In a marketing context, listening to the customer is a function through which we understand and adjust to the needs the customer is expressing. We listen to learn if our sales channels are clear. We listen to learn if our customers believe we are committed to after-sales service, and if that's reflected in what our customers are saying about the products they are getting through retail outlets. It turns out that these are only a few ways we use our listening skills to develop better sales and service. After all, nothing happens until somebody sells something.

The PR context is what we like to call organizational-public relationship development and management in order to differentiate it from one increasingly minor function of PR—generating publicity in the public media.

The role of PR extends far beyond (but includes) generating publicity for our organizations or clients. Public relations has the responsibility for collecting information from our various stakeholders and feeding that information into our organization with the intention of changing the behavior of our organization to better conform to the values and expectations of our stakeholders. Beyond the adjustment phase, PR also takes responsibility for letting these stakeholders know our organization is adjusting in order to have better relationships with them.

We listen and we learn—we always learn. If we don't, we may have heard our customers or other stakeholders, but we haven't been listening. The stethoscope is a tool that changed the face of medicine in the early 1800s when it first gave doctors the ability to hear what was going inside a body. The stories that it told helped doctors save lives.

In much the same way, the social media listening tools that are now freely available to every individual and organization can help reveal the mysteries of myriad relationships between businesses and their stakeholders.

If you have been paying attention and practicing, you now have an edge on your competition. Use this edge wisely, and don't forget to let us know how you're doing.

Visit our website and share your stories, and by all means, never hesitate to contact us directly. We're here for you.

Allie Siarto
http://twitter.com/allieo

Richard T. Cole
DrRichardCole@gmail.com

About the Authors

At age 24, **Allie Siarto** co-founded Loudpixel, a social media monitoring and research company that has redefined how companies approach market research. Rather than relying on expensive, time-consuming surveys or focus groups, Loudpixel helps companies better understand their customers by analyzing social media conversations that are already taking place each day. Loudpixel's research has been used by global Fortune 500 companies, marketing agencies and print publications to drive brand planning, product development, strategic communications, media buying, customer service and business strategies.

Outside of Loudpixel, Siarto teaches a class on monitoring and measuring social media as a part of Michigan State University's New Media Driver's License® course sequence. Her work has been published in Forbes, PC World, The Washington Post, Upstart Business Journal, Yahoo! Small Business Advisor, MSN, VentureBeat and Under 30 CEO.

Get in touch with Allie Siarto at:
http://twitter.com/allieo
http://loudpixel.com/contact
http://thecreativecareer.com
http://www.linkedin.com/in/allieosmar

Dr. Richard Cole (http://en.wikipedia.org/ wiki/Richard_T._Cole) is a recognized expert in PR—"organizational-public relationships." He has owned a PR company and a variety of other businesses. In the 1980s, Cole served as the press secretary and later as chief of staff to Michigan's Governor James J. Blanchard. For most of the next two decades, Cole headed up PR, marketing, strategy and other functions for America's largest inde-pendent nonprofit health plan, capping off his healthcare career as chief administrative offi-cer of a nine-hospital academic healthcare system in Detroit.

Cole is professor of public relations at Michigan State University, East Lansing, and recently completed an assignment as a member of the national Knowledge-to-Action Task Force on Child Maltreatment Prevention of the Centers for Disease Control and Prevention, Atlanta.

He is the author of a number of academic publications and is co-author, with Derek Mehraban, of *Google This: The New Media Driver's License®*, as well as the first edition of the resource guide.

While serving as chairperson of MSU's Department of Advertising, Public Relations and Retailing, Cole developed the New Media Driver's License® course sequence. He had invited Allie Siarto to speak to one of his graduate public relations classes, and it was this initial interaction that provided the inspiration for Cole to ask Siarto to create an advanced class for MSU in monitoring and analyzing conversations in social media. That class provided the inspiration for this book.

Cole lives in Haslett, Michigan, with his wife Deborah, a sculptor.

You can stay in touch with Rick at:
http://www.facebook.com/DrRichardCole
http://www.linkedin.com/pub/richard-t-cole/5/30b/a28
DrRichardCole@gmail.com

INDEX

Racom Communications Order Form

QUANTITY	TITLE	PRICE	AMOUNT
_____	The Social Current, **Allie Slarto/Richard T. Cole**	$24.95	_____
_____	Contemporary Direct & Interactive Marketing, 3rd Ed, **Lisa Spiller/Martin Baier**	$69.95	_____
_____	Google This: The New Media Driver's License® **Richard Cole/Derek Mehraban**	$24.95	_____
_____	Aligned, **Maurice Parisien**	$19.95	_____
_____	How to Jump-Start Your Career, **Robert L. Hemmings**	$19.95	_____
_____	This Year a Pogo Stick . . . Next Year a Unicycle, **Jim Kobs**	$19.95	_____
_____	Professional Selling, **Bill Jones**	$59.95	_____
_____	Follow That Customer, **Egbert Jan van Bel/Ed Sander/Alan Weber**	$39.95	_____
_____	Internet Marketing, **Herschell Gordon Lewis**	$19.95	_____
_____	Reliability Rules, **Don Schultz/Reg Price**	$34.95	_____
_____	The Marketing Performance Measurement Toolkit, **David M. Raab**	$39.95	_____
_____	Successful E-Mail Marketing Strategies, **Arthur M. Hughes/Arthur Sweetser**	$49.95	_____
_____	Managing Your Business Data, **Theresa Kushner/Maria Villar**	$32.95	_____
_____	Media Strategy and Planning Workbook, **DL Dickinson**	$64.95	_____
_____	Marketing Metrics in Action, **Laura Patterson**	$24.95	_____
_____	The IMC Handbook 3rd Edition, **J. Stephen Kelly/Susan K. Jones**	$49.95	_____
_____	Print Matters, **Randall Hines/Robert Lauterborn**	$27.95	_____
_____	The Business of Database Marketing, **Richard N. Tooker**	$49.95	_____
_____	Customer Churn, Retention, and Profitability, **Arthur Middleton Hughes**	$59.95	_____
_____	Data-Driven Business Models, **Alan Weber**	$49.95	_____
_____	Creative Strategy in Direct & Interactive Marketing, 4th Edition, **Susan K. Jones**	$49.95	_____
_____	Branding Iron, **Charlie Hughes and William Jeanes**	$27.95	_____
_____	Managing Sales Leads, **James Obermayer**	$39.95	_____
_____	Creating the Marketing Experience, **Joe Marconi**	$49.95	_____
_____	Brand Babble: Sense & Nonsense about Branding, **Don E. Schultz/Heidi F. Schultz**	$24.95	_____
_____	The New Marketing Conversation, **Donna Baier Stein/Alexandra MacAaron**	$34.95	_____
_____	Trade Show and Event Marketing, **Ruth Stevens**	$59.95	_____
_____	Sales & Marketing 365, **James Obermayer**	$17.95	_____
_____	Accountable Marketing, **Peter J. Rosenwald**	$59.95	_____
_____	Contemporary Database Marketing, Second Edition **Lisa Spiller/Kurtis Ruf**	$89.95	_____
_____	Catalog Strategist's Toolkit, **Katie Muldoon**	$59.95	_____
_____	Marketing Convergence, **Susan K. Jones/Ted Spiegel**	$34.95	_____
_____	High-Performance Interactive Marketing, **Christopher Ryan**	$39.95	_____
_____	The White Paper Marketing Handbook, **Robert W. Bly**	$39.95	_____
_____	Business-to-Business Marketing Research, **Martin Block/Tamara Block**	$69.95	_____
_____	Hot Appeals or Burnt Offerings, **Herschell Gordon Lewis**	$24.95	_____
_____	On the Art of Writing Copy, 4th Edition, **Herschell Gordon Lewis**	$34.95	_____
_____	Open Me Now, **Herschell Gordon Lewis**	$21.95	_____
_____	Marketing Mayhem, **Herschell Gordon Lewis**	$39.95	_____
_____	Asinine Advertising, **Herschell Gordon Lewis**	$22.95	_____

Name/Title_____

Company _____

Street Address _____

City/State/Zip _____

Email _____ Phone _____

Credit Card: ☐ VISA ☐ MasterCard
☐ American Express ☐ Discover

☐ Check or money order enclosed (payable to Racom
Communications in US dollars drawn on a US bank)

Subtotal _____

Subtotal from other side _____

8.65% Tax _____

Shipping & Handling _____
$7.00 for first book; $1.00
for each additional book.

TOTAL _____

Number _____ Exp. Date _____

Signature _____

Racom Communications, 150 N. Michigan Ave, Suite 2800, Chicago, IL 60601
312-494-0100, 800-247-6553, www. Racombooks.com

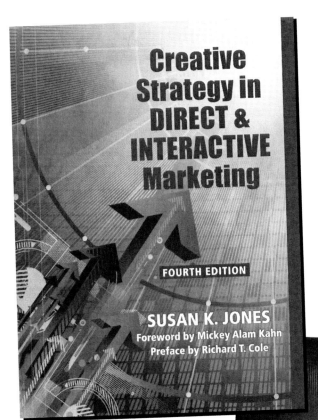

Creative Strategy in DIRECT & INTERACTIVE Marketing

FOURTH EDITION

SUSAN K. JONES
Foreword by Mickey Alam Kahn
Preface by Richard T. Cole

RĀCOM
COMMUNICATIONS

Contemporary Direct and Interactive Marketing

Third Edition

LISA D. SPILLER
MARTIN BAIER

IJ IMC

International Journal of Integrated Marketing Communications

VOLUME 5, NO. 1 | SPRING 2013

ARTICLES

Kelty Logan, University of Colorado at Boulder
Let's Make a Deal: The Exchange Value of Advertising

Lisa D. Spiller, Ph.D., Christopher Newport University
Using Metrics to Drive Integrated Marketing Communication Decisions: Hi-Ho Silver

William Ressler, Ithaca College
Integrating External Objectives with Internal Outcomes:
Benefits of Culturally Based, Holistic Approaches to IMC in Minor League Baseball

Stacy Neier, Loyola University Chicago and Drai Hassert, Sortis Internet Marketing
GREENOLAStyle: A Brand on a Mission

Victor A. Barger, University of Wisconsin–Whitewater; Lauren I. Labrecque, Loyola University Chicago
An Integrated Marketing Communications Perspective on Social Media Metrics

Amit Banerji, Maulana Azad National Institute of Technology;
Mohd Iqbal Khan, Barkatullah University; Mudasir Ahad Wani, Barkatullah Universit
India's New Language of Advertising: A Study of Change in Post-Libe

For subscription information, call Racom Communication
Or go to: http://www.IJIMC.com
ISSN: (print) 1943-3735; (online) 1943-374

RACOM
COMMUNICATIONS

2ND EDITION

The IMC HANDBOOK

Readings & Cases in Integrated Marketing Communications

J. STEVEN KELLY
SUSAN K. JONES